Background Knowledge for Academic Subjects

Fundamental
Reading

Rachel Somer

BASIC 1

DARAKWON

About the Author

Rachel Somer

BA in English Literature, York University, Toronto, Canada

Award-winning essayist, TOEIC developer, and author of educational books

Over ten years of experience as an English as a Second Language instructor

Fundamental Reading BASIC 1

Publisher Chung Kyudo
Author Rachel Somer
Editors Kim Minju, Jeong Yeonsoon, Kim Namyeon
Designers Park Narae, Black & White

First published in November 2019
By Darakwon, Inc.
Darakwon Bldg., 211, Munbal-ro, Paju-si, Gyeonggi-do 10881
Republic of Korea
Tel: 82-2-736-2031 (Ext. 250)
Fax: 82-2-732-2037

ISBN 978-89-277-0857-5 54740
978-89-277-0856-8 54740 (set)

www.darakwon.co.kr

Photo Credits
Tipwam (p. 38), Anton_Ivanov (p. 39), JStone (p. 40), Brian S (p. 54),
serato (p. 95), Tatiana SP & teamLab (pp. 102-103) / Shutterstock.com

Components Student Book / Workbook
12 11 10 9 8 7 6   24 25 26 27 28

Fundamental Reading

BASIC 1

DARAKWON

How to Use This Book

This book has 8 chapters that cover different academic subjects. Each chapter is composed of 2 units based on interesting topics related to the subject.

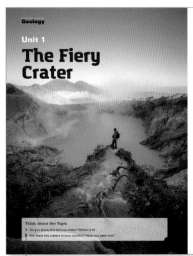

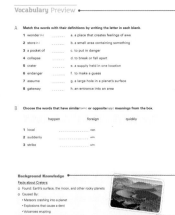

Vocabulary Preview

Students can learn the key words from the passage and get ready to read.

Background Knowledge

Students can read brief information that will help them predict and understand the main reading passage.

Think about the Topic

Two warm-up questions are provided to motivate students to think about the topic before continuing with the unit.

QR code for listening to the passage

Main Reading Passage

The passages discuss topics that have been carefully chosen to provide academic knowledge as well as to interest students. Each passage is between 200–230 words long.

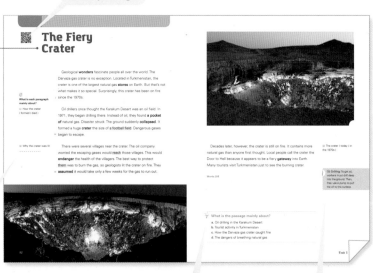

Finding the topic of each paragraph

Finding the main topic or main idea of the passage

Additional information and further learning about the topic

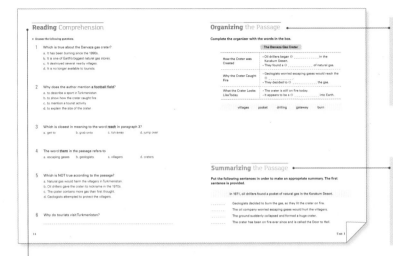

Organizing the Passage

By completing a graphic organizer, students can review and recognize important ideas and information presented in the passage.

Summarizing the Passage

Either by arranging sentences in the correct order or by completing a summary, students can review the main points of the passage once again.

Reading Comprehension

5 multiple-choice questions and 1 short-answer question are given to help students master various types of questions.

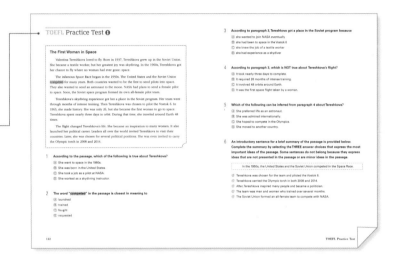

TOEFL Practice Test

At the end of the book, there is a supplementary TOEFL Practice Test section containing four passages. Each passage has six questions that frequently appear on real TOEFL tests.

Workbook

The first part contains 4 types of exercises, which provide students with a deeper understanding of the passage as well as enhanced vocabulary and language skills.

The second part presents a writing topic related to the reading passage. Students can develop their thoughts on the topic, conduct further research on their own, and learn to write a short paragraph.

Table of Contents

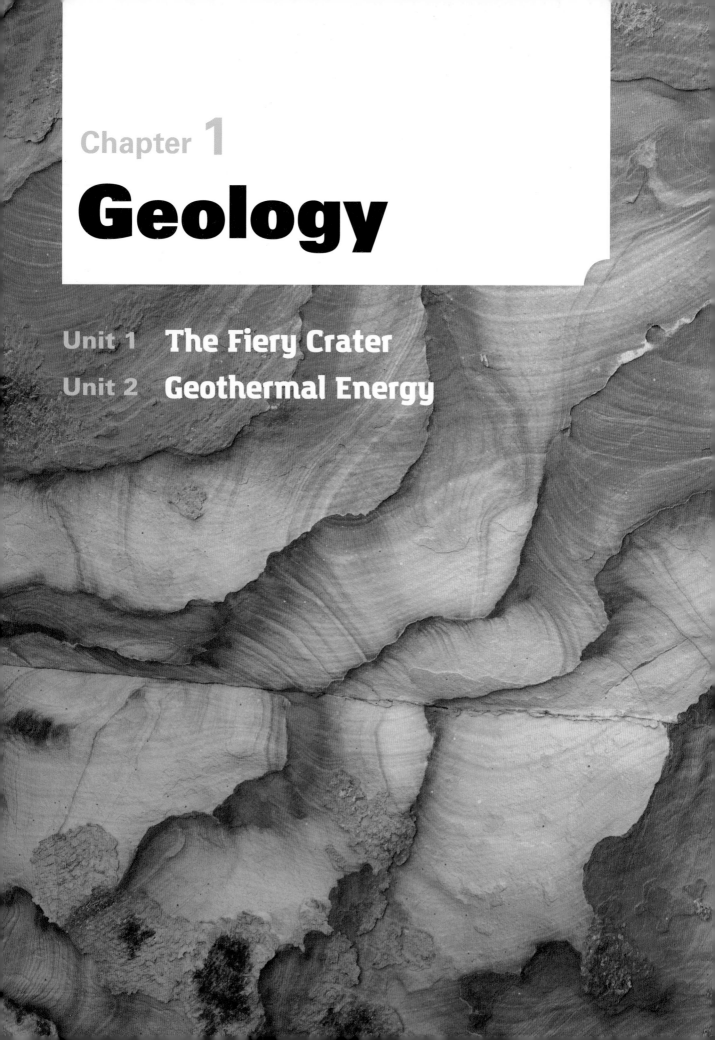

Chapter 1
Geology

Geology is the study of the Earth. Geologists examine rocks and other hard surfaces to determine how land formed. They try to predict what will happen to the land in the future.

Geology

Unit 1
The Fiery Crater

Think about the Topic

1 Do you know of a famous crater? Where is it?

2 Are there any craters in your country? Have you seen one?

Vocabulary Preview

A   Match the words with their definitions by writing the letter in each blank.

1 wonder *(n.)*   _____   a. a place that creates feelings of awe

2 store *(n.)*   _____   b. a small area containing something

3 a pocket of   _____   c. to put in danger

4 collapse   _____   d. to break or fall apart

5 crater   _____   e. a supply held in one location

6 endanger   _____   f. to make a guess

7 assume   _____   g. a large hole in a planet's surface

8 gateway   _____   h. an entrance into an area

B   Choose the words that have similar *(sim.)* or opposite *(opp.)* meanings from the box.

happen	foreign	quickly

1 local   _____ *opp.*

2 suddenly   _____ *sim.*

3 strike   _____ *sim.*

Background Knowledge

Facts about Craters:

- Found: Earth's surface, the moon, and other rocky planets
- Caused By:
  - Meteors crashing into a planet
  - Explosions that cause a dent
  - Volcanoes erupting

The Fiery Crater

Geological **wonders** fascinate people all over the world. The Darvaza gas crater is no exception. Located in Turkmenistan, the crater is one of the largest natural gas **stores** on Earth. But that's not what makes it so special. Surprisingly, this crater has been on fire
5 since the 1970s.

Oil drillers once thought the Karakum Desert was an oil field. In 1971, they began drilling there. Instead of oil, they found **a pocket of** natural gas. Disaster struck. The ground suddenly **collapsed**. It formed a huge **crater** the size of a football field. Dangerous gases
10 began to escape.

There were several villages near the crater. The oil company worried the escaping gases would reach those villages. This would **endanger** the health of the villagers. The best way to protect them was to burn the gas, so geologists lit the crater on fire. They
15 **assumed** it would take only a few weeks for the gas to run out.

Q
What is each paragraph mainly about?

P2 How the crater (formed / died)

P3 Why the crater was lit

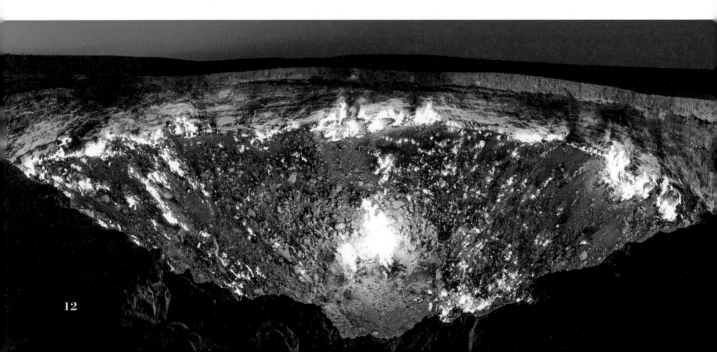

Decades later, however, the crater is still on fire. It contains more natural gas than anyone first thought. Local people call the crater the Door to Hell because it appears to be a fiery **gateway** into Earth. Many tourists visit Turkmenistan just to see the burning crater.

Words 203

 P4 The crater (today / in the 1970s)

> ℹ **Oil Drilling:** To get oil, workers must drill deep into the ground. Then, they use a pump to pull the oil to the surface.

 What is the passage mainly about?

a. Oil drilling in the Karakum Desert
b. Tourist activity in Turkmenistan
c. How the Darvaza gas crater caught fire
d. The dangers of breathing natural gas

Reading Comprehension

● **Answer the following questions.**

1   Which is true about the Darvaza gas crater?

   a. It has been burning since the 1990s.

   b. It is one of Earth's biggest natural gas stores.

   c. It destroyed several nearby villages.

   d. It is no longer available to tourists.

2   Why does the author mention a football field?

   a. to describe a sport in Turkmenistan

   b. to show how the crater caught fire

   c. to mention a tourist activity

   d. to explain the size of the crater

3   Which is closest in meaning to the word reach in paragraph 3?

   a. get to　　　　b. grab onto　　　　c. run away　　　　d. jump over

4   The word them in the passage refers to

   a. escaping gases　　b. geologists　　　c. villagers　　　d. craters

5   Which is NOT true according to the passage?

   a. Natural gas would harm the villagers in Turkmenistan.

   b. Oil drillers gave the crater its nickname in the 1970s.

   c. The crater contains more gas than first thought.

   d. Geologists attempted to protect the villagers.

6   Why do tourists visit Turkmenistan?

   _____

Organizing the Passage

Complete the organizer with the words in the box.

The Darvaza Gas Crater	
How the Crater was Created	• Oil drillers began ❶ _____ in the Karakum Desert. • They found a ❷ _____ of natural gas.
Why the Crater Caught Fire	• Geologists worried escaping gases would reach the ❸ _____. • They decided to ❹ _____ the gas.
What the Crater Looks Like Today	• The crater is still on fire today. • It appears to be a ❺ _____ into Earth.

villages	pocket	drilling	gateway	burn

Summarizing the Passage

Put the following sentences in order to make an appropriate summary. The first sentence is provided.

In 1971, oil drillers found a pocket of natural gas in the Karakum Desert.

_____ Geologists decided to burn the gas, so they lit the crater on fire.

_____ The oil company worried escaping gases would hurt the villagers.

_____ The ground suddenly collapsed and formed a huge crater.

_____ The crater has been on fire ever since and is called the Door to Hell.

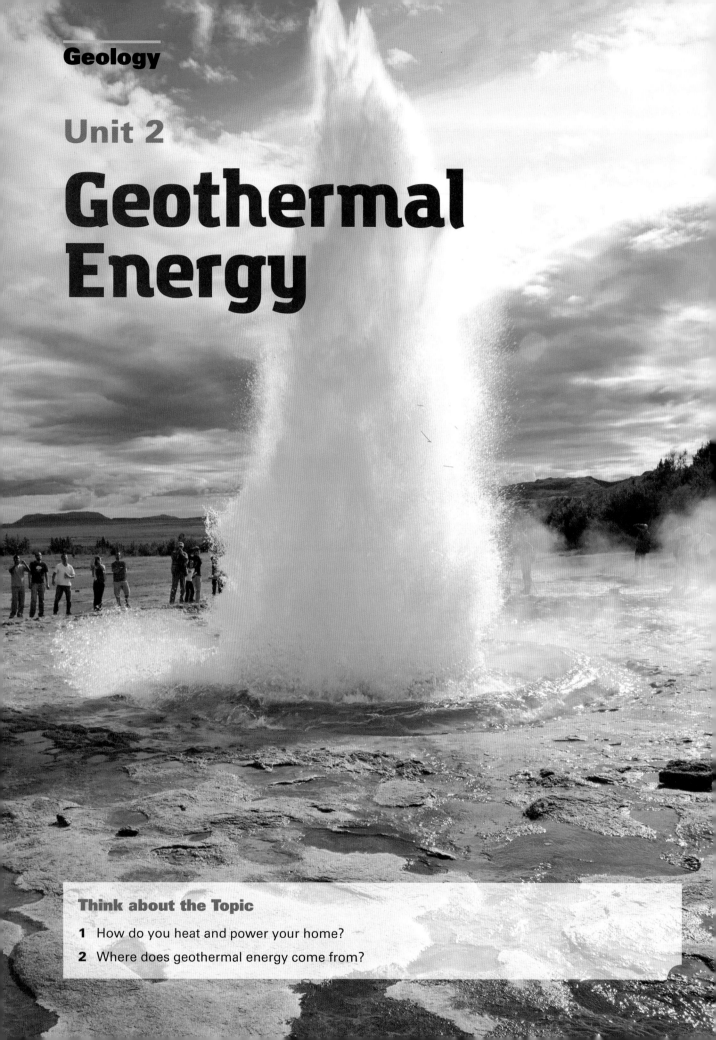

Unit 2

Geothermal Energy

Think about the Topic

1 How do you heat and power your home?

2 Where does geothermal energy come from?

Vocabulary Preview

A   **Match the words with their definitions by writing the letter in each blank.**

1 rely on   _____   a. to need for comfort or survival

2 pipe   _____   b. to place underground

3 bury   _____   c. a machine that spins

4 absorb   _____   d. a tube usually made of metal

5 cool *(v.)*   _____   e. leftover

6 pump *(v.)*   _____   f. to lower the temperature

7 turbine   _____   g. to push a liquid through a pipe

8 remaining   _____   h. to pull into

B   **Choose the words that have similar** *(sim.)* **or opposite** *(opp.)* **meanings from the box.**

below	useful	rotate

1 above   _____ *opp.*

2 spin   _____ *sim.*

3 beneficial   _____ *sim.*

Background Knowledge

Geothermal Power for Homes:

Powering a home can be very costly. It can also harm the environment in many ways. However, geothermal energy is a clean resource that can heat, cool, and power your home. Geothermal power plants use underground heat to create electricity.

Geothermal Energy

People **rely on** many types of energy to heat and power their homes. Geothermal energy is one of the cleanest resources on the planet. The word "geo" means "from Earth" and "thermal" means "heat." As the name suggests, this type of energy is found
5 underground. It can be used in a few interesting ways.

The temperature underground stays the same all year long. A geothermal heating system needs **pipes**. These are **buried** deep underground. A liquid is **pumped** through the pipes. There, it **absorbs** heat. Then it's pumped back above ground, usually into a home. The
10 heat is used to warm the air of the home.

The reverse is also possible. A geothermal system can **cool** a home during warmer months. Instead of bringing heat into the home, it absorbs the heat. Then it carries it back underground. These systems are energy efficient. This means the cost of heating and
15 cooling a home is very low.

Q

What is each paragraph mainly about?

P2 How geothermal energy _____ a home

P3 Geothermal systems in _____ months

Geothermal energy can also make electricity. Geothermal power plants pump cold water underground. This creates steam. The heat from the steam spins a **turbine**, which makes electricity. The electricity travels to homes. The **remaining** water is cooled, and the process begins again. Geothermal power plants are especially beneficial because they don't harm the environment.

Words 210

P4 How geothermal energy makes (water / electricity)

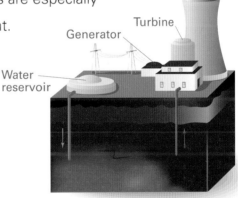

20

Steam

Turbine

Generator

Water reservoir

Check the main idea of the passage.

a. Geothermal energy can heat, cool, and power a home.
b. Geothermal power plants make clean energy.
c. Water absorbs heat when it is pumped underground.
d. Geothermal cooling systems are very cheap.

i Other Types of Energy:
Coal, natural gas, and nuclear power are the most common types of energy. Clean energy sources are generated by water, wind, and solar power.

Reading Comprehension

● **Answer the following questions.**

1 Which is true according to paragraph 1?

   a. Earth doesn't have much geothermal energy.

   b. Geothermal energy is found underground.

   c. People never use geothermal energy.

   d. Geothermal energy makes water dirty.

2 The word it in the passage refers to

   a. temperature   b. liquid   c. heat   d. pipe

3 Which is NOT mentioned as a way to use geothermal energy?

   a. cooling a home in summer

   b. heating a home in winter

   c. powering a home with electricity

   d. removing water from the air

4 What does the underlined part in the passage mean?

   a. Putting a geothermal heating system in a home is very cheap.

   b. Geothermal power plants are not expensive to build.

   c. The cost of heating a home is higher than the cost of cooling it.

   d. People don't pay a lot to use geothermal energy in their homes.

5 Which is true about geothermal power plants?

   a. They reuse a home's heat energy.

   b. They carry cool water to homes.

   c. They use turbines to make electricity.

   d. They pump hot air underground.

6 Why are geothermal power plants beneficial?

Organizing the Passage

Complete the organizer with the words in the box.

Geothermal Energy

How Geothermal Energy Heats a Home	• Geothermal ❶ _____ systems pump water underground where it ❷_____ heat.
Geothermal Systems in Warmer Months	• Geothermal ❸ _____ systems absorb heat and carry it back underground.
How Geothermal Energy Makes Electricity	• ❹ _____ plants use ❺ _____ and turbines to make electricity. • The plants send the electricity to homes.

steam	heating	cooling	absorbs	power

Summarizing the Passage

The following is a summary of the passage. Fill in the blanks with the appropriate words.

underground	systems	resource	warms	turbine

Geothermal energy is a clean ❶ _____ that is found underground. It can be used in a few ways. Geothermal heating ❷ _____ use pipes buried underground. A liquid absorbs heat and then travels back into a home. There, it ❸ _____ the air. This system can also cool a home in warmer months. Instead, it carries the heat back ❹ _____ . Geothermal power plants can make electricity by using steam to spin a ❺ _____ . This electricity travels to homes.

Chapter 2
Zoology

Zoology is the study of animals. Zoologists learn about animals, their behavior, and how they interact with the environment. Zoologists also care about endangered species. They think of ways to keep these species safe.

Unit 3
The Red Panda

Think about the Topic

1 Have you ever seen a red panda? Where was it?

2 What do red pandas look like?

Vocabulary Preview

A   **Match the words with their definitions by writing the letter in each blank.**

1 related to   _____   a. doing many things

2 marking   _____   b. being in the same family with someone

3 unique   _____   c. a pattern on an animal

4 native to   _____   d. belonging to one area

5 active   _____   e. special

6 herbivore   _____   f. the place an animal lives

7 habitat   _____   g. an animal that eats only plants

8 poaching   _____   h. the act of killing endangered species

B   **Choose the words that have similar** (*sim.*) **or opposite** (*opp.*) **meanings from the box.**

ordinary	mostly	like

1 prefer   _____ *sim.*

2 unique   _____ *opp.*

3 mainly   _____ *sim.*

Background Knowledge

Facts About Red Pandas:

○ Diet: Bamboo, fruits, bugs, eggs, birds

○ Size:

 • Weight: 5-9 kilograms

 • Length: around 60 cm

 • Long, fluffy tails

○ Markings: Black legs, ringed tails, white stripes on faces

The Red Panda

Q

What is each paragraph mainly about?

P1 The red panda's
(diet / appearance)

P2 (Markings / Habitat)
and food

P3 (Dangers / Areas) red
pandas face

Unlike the name suggests, red pandas aren't closely **related to** giant pandas. In fact, they look nothing like giant pandas. Red pandas have reddish brown fur and pointed ears. The **markings** on their faces and tails are similar to raccoons. However, red pandas are not
5 members of the raccoon family, either. ❶ Their **unique** appearance places them in their own special family.

Red pandas are **native to** the Himalayas and southwestern China. They prefer forested areas where they can climb and sleep in trees. ❷ Red pandas are known for lazily relaxing on tree branches during the
10 day. At night, they become **active**. Like giant pandas, red pandas eat mainly bamboo. But they are not true **herbivores**. ❸

The red panda is currently listed as an endangered species. There are fewer than 10,000 red pandas living in the wild. This is
15 mostly due to the destruction of their **habitat**. But **poaching** has also become a problem. ❹ In China, red pandas are hunted for their fur and fluffy tails.

Birth rates are low for red pandas. Females might give birth only once per year. This is not enough to sustain the population while poaching continues. India and China have made protected areas for red pandas. In these areas, poaching is illegal. But this does not always stop poachers from hunting. **Words 223**

20

PM Lowering
(population / poaching)

 What is the passage mainly about?

a. The life and habitat of the red panda
b. Why red pandas prefer to eat bamboo
c. How to increase the red panda's birth rate
d. Forest destruction in southwestern China

ℹ **Red Panda Population:** No one is sure how many red pandas are living in the wild. In 2008, red pandas were listed as endangered because there are fewer than 10,000 living in the wild. However, that number may be much lower now.

Reading Comprehension

● **Answer the following questions.**

1 Which is NOT true about the daily lives of red pandas?

   a. They live in groups of three to five.

   b. They become more active at night.

   c. They climb and sleep in trees.

   d. They prefer to eat mostly bamboo.

2 Which is true about poaching in China?

   a. Red pandas are killed for their fur and tails.

   b. Poaching is no longer a problem in this region.

   c. There are fewer than 10,000 poachers in China.

   d. Only female red pandas are being hunted.

3 Where would the following sentence best fit in the passage?

They also eat eggs, birds, and insects.

   a. ❶   b. ❷   c. ❸   d. ❹

4 What can you guess about poachers?

   a. They only hunt in protected areas.

   b. They are usually caught and put in jail.

   c. They are breaking laws to hunt red pandas.

   d. They prefer to hunt in India rather than China.

5 Which is closest in meaning to the word currently in paragraph 3?

   a. quietly   b. wildly   c. unfortunately   d. presently

6 What did India and China make for red pandas?

   _____

Organizing the Passage

Complete the organizer with the words in the box.

The Red Panda	
The Red Panda's Appearance	• They have reddish brown fur and ❶ _____ ears. • Markings on their faces and tails are similar to raccoons.
❷ _____ and Food	• They are native to the Himalayas and China. • They prefer ❸ _____ areas.
Dangers Red Pandas Face	• They are hunted for their fur and ❹ _____. • Their habitats are destroyed.
Lowering Population	• Birth rates are too low to ❺ _____ their population. • Poachers continue to hunt them.

tails	sustain	pointed	habitat	forested

Summarizing the Passage

The following is a summary of the passage. Fill in the blanks with the appropriate words.

appearance	protected	fewer	members	destruction

Red pandas are not ❶ _____ of the giant panda or raccoon families. Their unique ❷ _____ puts them in their own family. Native to the Himalayas and China, red pandas prefer forested areas. They relax during the day but become active at night. There are ❸ _____ than 10,000 red pandas alive. This is due to the ❹ _____ of their habitat as well as poaching. Also, birth rates are very low for red pandas. India and China have made ❺ _____ areas for them. However, poaching still continues.

Unit 4
Crow Intelligence

Think about the Topic

1 What are the smartest animals?

2 Where can you normally see crows? What do they look like?

Vocabulary Preview

A **Match the words with their definitions by writing the letter in each blank.**

1 swoop _____ a. a display of anger

2 reputation _____ b. the opinions held about someone or something

3 clever _____ c. very smart

4 socialize _____ d. to attempt to beat someone at something

5 compete _____ e. to react to someone or something

6 encounter (n.) _____ f. to move downward very quickly

7 aggression _____ g. to interact with others

8 respond _____ h. an experience

B **Choose the words that have similar** (sim.) **or opposite** (opp.) **meanings from the box.**

meanness	smart	forget

1 remember _____ opp.

2 intelligent _____ sim.

3 kindness _____ opp.

Background Knowledge

The Smartest Animals:

Many animal species are known for being very intelligent. Crows are thought to be the smartest birds. They are able to form complex relationships with each other. They are also clever enough to use simple tools.

Crow Intelligence

Q

What is each paragraph mainly about?

 P1 The story of

_____ .

In 2011, four-year-old Gabi Mann accidentally dropped a chicken nugget. A hungry crow **swooped** in to steal it. Soon, other crows came to Gabi for food. Then an incredible
5 thing happened. The crows began leaving gifts. Over the years, Gabi's collection of gifts grew. She was certain these birds were thanking her for feeding them.

P2 The (intelligence / bodies) of crows

Many people have stories similar to Gabi's. Crows now have a **reputation** for being very intelligent. Some species of crow are even
10 **clever** enough to use tools. They use long sticks to dig for insects. They also use stones to crack open nuts. Scientists believe they owe their intelligence to their brain size. A crow's brain is quite large compared to the rest of its body.

P3 How crows

_____

Crows are also known for having excellent memories. This may be
15 due to the way they **socialize** with each other. Young crows often live together in large groups. They **compete** with other members of the group as they look for a mate. They store information about these relationships.

This ability extends to humans as well. Crows remember the **encounters** they have with humans. They remember kindness. They may repay it by leaving gifts. _____, crows also remember **aggression**. They may **respond** negatively when a human is unkind or violent. Words 210

P4 (Kindness / Relationships) with humans

 Check the main idea of the passage.

a. Crows compete with other members of their group.

b. Crows are able to use tools to look for food.

c. Crows give gifts to humans who are kind to them.

d. Crows are intelligent and have great memories.

i **Crow Communication:** Crows have their own unique sort of language. They use various sounds to communicate about specific events.

Reading Comprehension

• **Answer the following questions.**

1   Why does the author mention Gabi Mann in paragraph 1?

    a   To explain why crows are the smartest birds

    b. To illustrate how crows respond to kindness

    c. To give an example of crow aggression

    d. To describe where to find crows

2   Which is true according to paragraph 2?

    a. The brain of a crow is considered large.

    b. Crows use stones to dig for insects.

    c. Scientists cannot study the tools crows use.

    d. Crows have larger bodies than other birds.

3   The word They in the passage refers to

    a. Scientists   b. People   c. Young crows   d. Memories

4   What does the underlined part in the passage mean?

    a. Young crows have trouble remembering things.

    b. Not much is known about crow relationships.

    c. Crows remember their relationships with others.

    d. The smartest crows have the best relationships.

5   Which is the best choice for the blank?

    a. Because   b. However   c. Regardless   d. Since

6   What might crows do when a human is unkind?

34

Organizing the Passage

Complete the organizer with the words in the box.

Crow Intelligence	
The Story of Gabi Mann	• Crows came to Gabi for food. • They began leaving ❶ _____ to thank her.
The Intelligence of Crows	• They use ❷ _____ to find food. • Their brains are large for their bodies.
How Crows Socialize	• They ❸ _____ with each other for mates. • They store ❹ _____ about these relationships.
Relationships with Humans	• Crows repay ❺ _____ and remember aggression.

information	tools	gifts	kindness	compete

Summarizing the Passage

Put the following sentences in order to make an appropriate summary. The first sentence is provided.

Crows have a reputation for being very clever.

_____ Crows will also remember the kindness and aggression of humans.

_____ Crows are also known for having very good memories.

_____ They remember how they compete with other crows in their group.

_____ Scientists think this is because of their brain size.

Chapter 3
Literature

Literature is a collection of written works, such as books and poetry. Literature may be fiction or non-fiction. People read literature for enjoyment. They also study it to learn more about history, culture, and society.

Unit 5
J.K. Rowling's Impact

Think about the Topic

1 What do you think of the *Harry Potter* series?

2 Who is your favorite *Harry Potter* character?

Vocabulary Preview

A **Match the words with their definitions by writing the letter in each blank.**

1 merchandise _____ a. items that are bought and sold

2 poverty _____ b. to start an organization

3 charity _____ c. the state of being very poor

4 found _____ d. the state of being kind and giving

5 generosity _____ e. a story written by a fan about a published work

6 pop culture _____ f. art and beliefs that are popular at a given time

7 fanfiction _____ g. a group of people born around the same time

8 generation _____ h. an organization that raises money for the poor

B **Choose the words that have similar** *(sim.)* **or opposite** *(opp.)* **meanings from the box.**

create	successful	publish

1 release _____ *sim.*

2 failed _____ *opp.*

3 found _____ *sim.*

Background Knowledge

Facts About *Harry Potter*:

- Author: J.K. Rowling
- Genre: Fantasy
- Published: June 1997 – July 2007
- Main Characters: Harry, Ron, Hermione, Professor Dumbledore, Voldemort
- Adaptations:
  - An 8-part film series by Warner Bros. Pictures
  - A play co-written by Rowling

J.K. Rowling's Impact

People all over the world celebrate *Harry Potter*. Whether they watch the films, read the books, visit *Harry Potter* theme parks, or purchase Hogwarts

5 **merchandise**, people of all ages can enjoy the world and characters. But who is the woman behind the *Harry Potter* brand?

▲ J.K. Rowling © JStone

Q

What is each paragraph mainly about?

P2 Rowling's (hardships / childhood)

Joanne Rowling, known as J.K.

10 Rowling, didn't always have a glamorous life. While she wrote the first *Harry Potter* novel, her mother died suddenly. Rowling was also living in **poverty** after a failed marriage. But she never gave up writing. In 1997, the first *Harry Potter* novel was published. Six sequels were released.

P3 Rowling's
_____

15 The books sold over 500 million copies. J.K. Rowling became the world's first billionaire author. She used her success for good by donating to many **charities**. She even **founded** her own. Rowling's **gencrosity** caused her to lose her billionaire status, but that didn't stop her. She continued to help

20   those less fortunate.

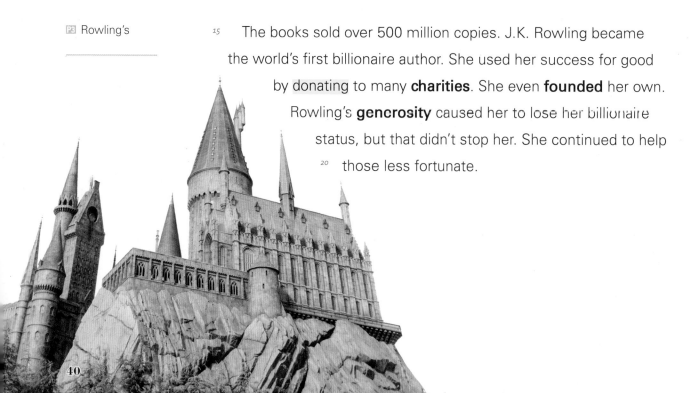

Rowling impacted the world in many ways. *Harry Potter* turned into a **pop culture** phenomenon. Although the series was geared toward children, fans young and old dreamed of attending Hogwarts. They wrote their own **fanfiction** and held *Harry Potter*-themed parties. Many even chose Hogwarts houses to join. Decades later, *Harry Potter* remains popular. It has even reached the next **generation** of young readers. **Words 213**

P4 Rowling's
_____ on the
world

25

i Intended Audience:
Harry Potter is a middle grade series aimed at 9–12-year-olds. However, as the series progressed, the books got longer and more mature.

 What is the passage mainly about?

a. J.K. Rowling's early life and education

b. *Harry Potter*'s influence on young authors

c. How to overcome hardships as an author

d. J.K. Rowling's success and effect on the world

Reading Comprehension

- **Answer the following questions.**

1   Which is NOT a way people celebrate *Harry Potter*?

    a. They buy Hogwarts merchandise.

    b. They go to *Harry Potter* amusement parks.

    c. They write letters to their favorite characters.

    d. They read the books and watch the films.

2   Which is true about J.K. Rowling's life while she was writing *Harry Potter*?

    a. Her husband helped her write.

    b. She was already a billionaire.

    c. She was living a glamorous life.

    d. Her mother died suddenly.

3   Which is closest in meaning to the word donating in paragraph 3?

    a. receiving   b. giving   c. collecting   d. surviving

4   What does the underlined part in the passage mean?

    a. J.K. Rowling's books became popular among young people.

    b. The *Harry Potter* films were more popular than the books.

    c. J.K. Rowling achieved her popularity because of the Internet.

    d. *Harry Potter* fanfiction has changed the way books are sold.

5   The word They in paragraph 4 refers to

    a. Children   b. Fans   c. Series   d. Charities

6   How many books in the *Harry Potter* series did J.K. Rowling sell?

Organizing the Passage

Complete the organizer with the words in the box.

J.K. Rowling's Impact

Rowling's ❶ _____	• Rowling was living in ❷ _____ after a failed marriage. • Her mother died suddenly, but she did not give up writing.
Rowling's Success	• Rowling became the world's first ❸ _____ author. • She donated to charities and ❹ _____ her own.
Rowling's Impact on the World	• *Harry Potter* became a pop culture phenomenon and remains popular decades later. • Fans of all ages dream of ❺ _____ Hogwarts.

founded	billionaire	attending	poverty	hardships

Summarizing the Passage

Put the following sentences in order to make an appropriate summary. The first sentence is provided.

People of all ages enjoy *Harry Potter*, but who is J.K. Rowling, the author behind this famous brand?

_____ However, she never gave up, and the books brought her huge success.

_____ Rowling used her success for good and donated a lot of money.

_____ Decades later, *Harry Potter* remains popular among readers of all ages.

_____ J.K. Rowling was living in poverty when she wrote *Harry Potter*.

Unit 6

From Science Fiction to Science Fact

Think about the Topic

1 What is your favorite science fiction book or film?

2 What fictional technology do you want to be real?

Vocabulary Preview

A   **Match the words with their definitions by writing the letter in each blank.**

1 imagine _____   a. a long work of fiction

2 gadget _____   b. an electronic machine

3 reality _____   c. to make a guess about the future

4 design (n.) _____   d. the state of being real

5 predict _____   e. to think of

6 purchase (v.) _____   f. without wires or cords

7 novel _____   g. a plan for a building, vehicle, or machine

8 wireless _____   h. to buy

B   **Choose the words that have similar (sim.) or opposite (opp.) meanings from the box.**

later	change	simple

1 turn into _____ sim.

2 soon _____ opp.

3 complex _____ opp.

Background Knowledge

Science Fiction:

   Science fiction, also called sci-fi, is an imaginative literary genre. Sci-fi is often set in the future. It often features fictional technologies and space travel. Science fiction authors use scientific ideas to create their fictional worlds and gadgets.

From Science Fiction to Science Fact

Q

What is each paragraph mainly about?

P2 _____
inspired Simon Lake

What will the future be like? Science fiction authors think about this question a lot. They **imagine** new **gadgets**. These gadgets make stories more exciting. But sometimes, these ideas inspire inventors who turn them into a **reality**.

5   Jules Verne was a famous French author. Verne's characters often went on exciting adventures in a submarine. This submarine was powered by electricity. At the time, there were various **designs** for real submarines. But none were as complex as Verne's. Verne's work inspired Simon Lake, who worked for the US navy. He built his first
10 submarine in 1894.

P3 Isaac Asimov
(invented / predicted)
self-driving cars

Over fifty years ago, Isaac Asimov wrote about a new type of car. In an essay, he **predicted** that cars would have robot brains. These cars would take humans where they needed to go. We can't **purchase** self-driving cars yet. However, many companies are testing
15 their own designs. Cars with robot brains may be on the road soon.

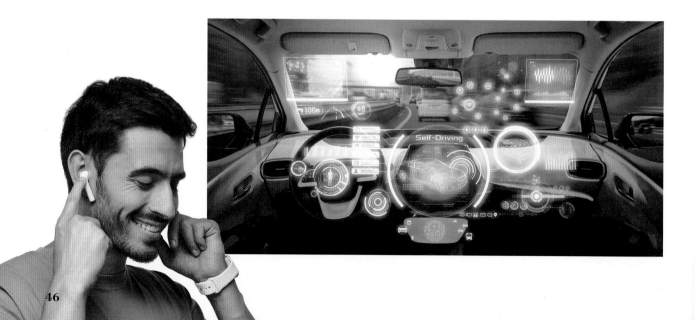

Author Ray Bradbury may have imagined the first *earbuds. In his **novel** *Fahrenheit 451*, Bradbury wrote about a gadget worn inside the ear. This gadget sent sound directly into the ear. This idea is similar to earbuds. Today, people use earbuds to listen to music or even make phone calls. **Wireless** earbuds are also becoming popular. Words 209 [20]

P4 _____
imagined the first
earbuds

*earbuds: headphones worn inside the ear

 Isaac Asimov: Isaac Asimov (1920–1992) is considered one of the fathers of science fiction. Asimov's stories have been translated widely and some have even been made into films.

Check the main idea of the passage.

a. Jules Verne had a greater impact than Ray Bradbury.
b. Most vehicles were inspired by science fiction.
c. Science fiction predicts and inspires new gadgets.
d. Wireless technology is becoming more popular.

Reading Comprehension

- **Answer the following questions.**

1 The word **them** in paragraph 1 refers to

    a. inventors   b. ideas   c. authors   d. stories

2 What can you guess about Simon Lake?

    a. He wrote his own science fiction stories.

    b. He read some of Jules Verne's work.

    c. His submarine was based on Asimov's design.

    d. His career with the US navy ended early.

3 Which is NOT true about self-driving cars?

    a. Isaac Asimov predicted them in an essay.

    b. They might be available to drive soon.

    c. Drivers can purchase them in some places.

    d. Companies are currently testing them.

4 Which is closest in meaning to the word **similar** in paragraph 4?

    a. unsure   b. exact   c. interesting   d. alike

5 Why docs the author mention **earbuds** in paragraph 4?

    a. To explain Jules Verne's idea in detail

    b. To predict a new type of gadget worn in ears

    c. To mention a gadget inspired by science fiction

    d. To describe the plot of a science fiction novel

6 What did Jules Verne's characters often do?

Organizing the Passage

Complete the organizer with the words in the box.

From Science Fiction to Science Fact	
Jules Verne	• He wrote about exciting ❶ _____ in a submarine. • His work ❷ _____ Simon Lake to build a submarine.
Isaac Asimov	• He predicted that cars would have ❸ _____ brains. • Companies are testing their own self-driving cars.
Ray Bradbury	• He may have imagined the first ❹ _____. • He wrote about a gadget that sent ❺ _____ into the ear.

| robot | adventures | inspired | sound | earbuds |

Summarizing the Passage

The following is a summary of the passage. Fill in the blanks with the appropriate words.

| imagine | self-driving | wrote | earbuds | electricity |

Science fiction authors ❶ _____ new gadgets. Sometimes, these ideas inspire inventors. Jules Verne wrote about a submarine that was powered by ❷ _____.
His work inspired Simon Lake to build a submarine in 1894. Over 50 years ago, Isaac Asimov ❸ _____ about cars with robot brains. Many companies are testing ❹ _____ cars now. These cars may be on the road soon. Ray Bradbury wrote about a gadget that sent sound into the ear. This idea is similar to ❺ _____.

Chapter 4
Environmental Science

Environmental science is the study of Earth's environment. Environmental scientists must have knowledge of many scientific fields, such as biology, chemistry, zoology, and more. They study how various processes affect the Earth.

Unit 7
Floating Trash Islands

Think about the Topic

1 How do you throw away plastic?

2 What can you do to reduce pollution?

Vocabulary Preview

A **Match the words with their definitions by writing the letter in each blank.**

1 accumulate _____   a. to take out

2 island _____   b. to lower an amount

3 drift _____   c. a body of land surrounded by water

4 piece _____   d. to float

5 devastating _____   e. to fix something

6 solve _____   f. to gather in one place

7 reduce _____   g. extremely harmful

8 remove _____   h. a small part of something

B **Choose the words that have similar** (*sim.*) **or opposite** (*opp.*) **meanings from the box.**

collect	transport	increase

1 reduce _____ *opp.*

2 accumulate _____ *sim.*

3 carry _____ *sim.*

Background Knowledge

The Effects of Plastic Pollution:

Plastic pollution is a major environmental problem. Millions of tonnes of plastic get into Earth's oceans. There, it breaks down into smaller pieces. This can poison the water supply. Many sea animals eat the plastic. They are unable to digest it and usually die.

Floating Trash Islands

Q

What is each paragraph mainly about?

P1 The (amount / location) of plastic trash

What happens to plastic when you throw it away? More and more, this trash ends up in rivers, which carry the plastic directly to Earth's
5 oceans. Approximately 2.4 million tonnes of plastic makes its way into the oceans every year. This trash has **accumulated** and formed floating **islands** of garbage.

▲ Kota Kinabalu Borneo in 2019 © Brian S

P2 The Great Pacific _____ Patch

The Great Pacific Garbage Patch is one of the largest of these
10 plastic islands. It can be found **drifting** in the Pacific Ocean. Much of the trash comes from countries in Asia. It has gathered between California and Hawaii. Currently, the island is three times bigger than France. It grows wider each year. More than 1.8 trillion **pieces** of plastic can be found here.

P3 A garbage patch in the (Atlantic / Pacific) Ocean

15 Another patch of ocean garbage can be found in the Atlantic Ocean. This trash island is hundreds of kilometers wide. Its effect on

sea life has been **devastating**. Many marine animals die after eating plastic. This can harm humans when they eat fish.

There may be hope for the oceans. It might be possible to **solve** the problem. We can start by **reducing** the amount of plastic we use. It's also important to _____ the oceans. Wildlife organizations are working on ways to safely **remove** the plastic.

20

P4 Possible (solutions / organizations)

Words 202

i **Plastic Waste Exporting:**
Although most ocean plastic comes from Asia, the plastic may have been shipped there. Many developed nations send their plastic trash to Asia instead of recycling it themselves.

 Check the main idea of the passage.

    a. Plastic trash has gathered in oceans to form islands.

    b. Pollution begins in oceans and spreads to other places.

    c. Plastic trash is most harmful to land and ocean animals.

    d. Wildlife organizations have a plan to clean up the oceans.

Reading Comprehension

● **Answer the following questions.**

1   How much trash gets into oceans every year?
   a. Less than 2 million tonnes
   b. Around 2.4 million tonnes
   c. About 1.8 trillion pieces
   d. Over 2 trillion pieces

2   Which is NOT mentioned about the Great Pacific Garbage Patch?
   a. It is currently three times bigger than France.
   b. It can be found between California and Hawaii.
   c. Fish are attracted to the colors of the plastic.
   d. Most of the trash comes from countries in Asia.

3   What happens to animals that eat plastic?
   a. They make their homes in the trash.
   b. Most of them only eat it once or twice.
   c. They are easy for fishermen to catch.
   d. Many of them die after eating it.

4   Which is closest in meaning to the word harm in paragraph 3?
   a. break   b. hurt   c. fix   d. starve

5   Which is the best choice for the blank?
   a. clean up   b. turn down   c. wake up   d. hand out

6   How big is the trash island in the Atlantic Ocean?

_____

Organizing the Passage

Complete the organizer with the words in the box.

Floating Trash Islands

The Amount of Plastic Trash	• Plastic trash has accumulated and formed ❶ _____ islands. • Around 2.4 million tonnes gets into oceans every year.
The Great Pacific Garbage Patch	• The garbage patch is three times ❷ _____ than France. • It contains more than 1.8 trillion ❸ _____ of plastic.
A Garbage Patch in the Atlantic Ocean	• This trash island is hundreds of kilometers wide. • It can harm ❹ _____ animals and humans.
Possible ❺ _____	• We can reduce the amount of plastic we use. • We can also clean up the oceans.

pieces	solutions	floating	marine	bigger

Summarizing the Passage

The following is a summary of the passage. Fill in the blanks with the appropriate words.

oceans	between	formed	problem	largest

Plastic trash has accumulated in oceans and ❶ _____ islands of garbage.
The Great Pacific Garbage Patch is the ❷ _____ of these islands. It can be found
drifting ❸ _____ California and Hawaii. It's three times bigger than France and
grows wider each year. Plastic is devastating to marine life, but there may be a way to solve
the ❹ _____ . We can reduce the amount of plastic we use as well as clean up the
❺ _____ .

Environmental Science

Unit 8
Desertification

Think about the Topic

1 What are the features of a desert?

2 How does an area of land become a desert?

Vocabulary Preview

A **Match the words with their definitions by writing the letter in each blank.**

1 man-made _____ a. a dangerous event caused by nature

2 graze _____ b. when land becomes covered in water

3 major _____ c. to eat grass and plants

4 drought _____ d. a lack of water

5 hunger _____ e. not using up resources

6 natural disaster _____ f. important or significant

7 flood _____ g. a feeling caused by a lack of food

8 sustainable _____ h. made by humans

B **Choose the words that have similar (*sim.*) or opposite (*opp.*) meanings from the box.**

	key	aquatic	sink

1 major _____ *sim.*

2 float _____ *opp.*

3 marine _____ *sim.*

Background Knowledge

<u>Types of Deserts:</u>

○ Hot and Dry Deserts: Hot in the day and freezing at night with very little rainfall

○ Cold Winter Deserts: Dry summers and winters with brief rainfall

○ Coastal Deserts: Long warm summers with only 3–6 cm of rain per year

○ Polar Deserts: Located at Earth's poles and always cool

Desertification

Q

What is each paragraph mainly about?

P1 How _____ form

P2 _____ of desertification

P3 (Causes / Effects) of desertification

Deserts are areas of dry, dusty land. They form when land loses its water, plants, and wildlife. This process is called desertification. Much of the world's land may become deserts in the near future. This will harm human life in many ways.

5　**Man-made** activities often cause desertification. Sometimes, farmers let too many animals **graze** in one area. This makes it hard for plants to grow. Cutting down trees is another **major** cause. When trees are cut down, other wildlife may die. Climate change is also a cause. As Earth warms, **droughts** occur more often. This causes
10　more areas to become deserts.

Desertification has many harmful effects. Firstly, it makes farming more difficult. This means not enough food will grow. Food prices will increase along with poverty and **hunger**. Secondly, desertification kills plants. Plants keep water clean, so drinking water will not be as
15　safe. Finally, deserts often experience **natural disasters**. Without plants, **floods** and dust storms will happen more often.

There are a few ways to prevent desertification. New laws for land use have helped. Education might also help. Farmers are learning **sustainable** farming methods. In some cases, desertification may even be reversed. <u>New technology may bring life and water back to deserts</u>. However, this takes a lot of time and money. **Words 212**

20

 P4 Ways to
_____ and
reverse desertification

i **Sustainable Farming:** Sustainable farming is farming that does not destroy the quality of the land. Farmers work to understand ecosystems and preserve them for future generations.

 What is the passage mainly about?

a. Reversing desertification with new technology
b. Causes, effects, and prevention of desertification
c. How climate change causes desertification
d. Ways in which desertification affects human life

Reading Comprehension

● **Answer the following questions.**

1   The word **This** in paragraph 1 refers to

     a. Wildlife   b. Desertification   c. Land   d. Plants

2   Why does the author mention grazing in paragraph 2?

     a. To name an activity that causes desertification

     b. To explain why farming may stop desertification

     c. To give an example of climate change

     d. To illustrate how sustainable farming works

3   Which is NOT mentioned as a cause of desertification?

     a. Cutting down trees   b. Farming

     c. Climate change   d. Storms

4   Which is true about plants according to paragraph 3?

     a. They are the first to die during desertification.

     b. They make drinking water safer to consume.

     c. They make grazing difficult for animals.

     d. They are expensive during floods and storms.

5   What does the underlined part in the passage mean?

     a. Farmers are using technology to protect their land.

     b. It is impossible to grow new plants in desert areas.

     c. Animals will return to deserts in the near future.

     d. Technology could help reverse desertification.

6   What happens as Earth warms?

Organizing the Passage

Complete the organizer with the words in the box.

Desertification	
How Deserts Form	• They form when land loses its water, plants, and ❶ _____.
Causes of Desertification	• Activities, such as farming and cutting down trees, cause desertification. • Climate change causes ❷ _____.
❸ _____ of Desertification	• Plants die and farming becomes difficult. • Natural ❹ _____ happen more often.
Ways to Reverse Desertification	• Education and new laws for land use may help. • Farmers can learn sustainable farming ❺ _____.

wildlife	effects	droughts	disasters	methods

Summarizing the Passage

Put the following sentences in order to make an appropriate summary. The first sentence is provided.

Deserts form when land loses its water, plants, and wildlife.

_____ Natural disasters, like floods, might also happen more frequently.

_____ Laws, education, and technology can help prevent desertification.

_____ Man-made activities and climate change cause areas to become deserts.

_____ When this happens, farming becomes more difficult and hunger will increase.

Chapter 5
Botany

Botany, a branch of biology, is the study of plant life. Botanists study the structures of plants and their processes. They also study the diseases that affect plant life. Botanists try to determine how plant life interacts with the environment.

Unit 9
Plants that Stink

Vocabulary Preview

A   **Match the words with their definitions by writing the letter in each blank.**

1 lure _____   a. to break down

2 disgusting _____   b. gross or terrible

3 rot _____   c. to not die

4 normally _____   d. to capture

5 seed _____   e. to attract

6 trap _____   f. a powdery substance that comes from a plant

7 pollen _____   g. usually

8 survive _____   h. something that can grow into an entire plant

B   **Choose the words that have similar** (*sim.*) **or opposite** (*opp.*) **meanings from the box.**

horrible	sugary	pull

1 attract   _____ *sim.*

2 sweet   _____ *sim.*

3 terrible   _____ *sim.*

Background Knowledge

- Titan Arum:
  - Largest flower in the world
  - Blooms once every 2–7 years but can live for up to 40 years
- Stinking Corpse Lily:
  - Heavy, wide, and maroon-colored
  - Grows as a parasite on the vines of other plants
- Dead Horse Arum Lily:
  - Can raise its own temperature to attract flies

Plants that Stink

When we think of flowers, we often imagine sweet scents that **lure** insects. But some flowering plants produce terrible smells. To humans, these smells may be **disgusting**. However, just like sweet-smelling plants, stinky plants also attract insects.

Q

What is each paragraph mainly about?

P2 The _____ Arum

5 The Titan Arum is one of the world's biggest flowers. Native to the rainforests of Sumatra in Indonesia, it can grow up to 3 meters tall. The Titan Arum is known as a "corpse flower." It gets this name because it produces a smell that's similar to **rotting** meat. Beetles and flies, which **normally** feed on decaying flesh, are attracted to 10 this smell.

P3 The (Heavy / Stinking) Corpse Lily

The Stinking Corpse Lily also grows in Indonesia. Unlike the Titan Arum, this flower is heavy and wide. It can weigh up to 11 kilograms. It also produces a smell like rotting meat. Forest animals and insects are attracted to the smell. They carry the flower's **seeds** to other 15 areas of the forest.

P4 The _____ Horse Arum Lily

As its name suggests, the Dead Horse Arum Lily smells like a dead horse. Flies are attracted to its terrible smell. The flower **traps** the flies inside it. Over the course of a day, 20 it covers the flies in **pollen**.

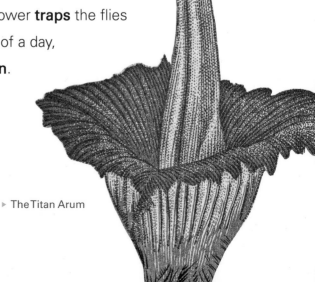

▶ The Titan Arum

▲ The Stinking Corpse Lily

When the flies are released, they carry the pollen to other Dead Horse Arum Lilies. This cross-pollination ensures the plant **survives** in the wild. Words 217

▶ The Dead Horse Arum Lily

 Check the main idea of the passage.

a. Most corpse flowers smell like dead horses.

b. Some plants produce terrible smells to lure insects.

c. Beetles carry seeds across large patches of land.

d. Flowers with sweet scents are common in rainforests.

i Cross-Pollination: Cross-pollination happens when pollen is transferred from one plant to another. The seeds that are created will have characteristics of both plants.

Reading Comprehension

● **Answer the following questions.**

1   Which is closest in meaning to the word produce in paragraph 1?

   a. invent   b. make   c. remove   d. agree

2   Which is NOT true about the Titan Arum?

   a. It is a wide and heavy flower.
   b. It attracts beetles and flies.
   c. It can grow up to 3 meters tall.
   d. It can be found in Indonesia.

3   Which is mentioned about the Stinking Corpse Lily?

   a. Its smell attracts other lilies.
   b. It makes a rotting meat smell.
   c. It grows in many different forests.
   d. It's the world's tallest flower.

4   Which is true about forest animals according to paragraph 3?

   a. They get trapped inside a plant's flower.
   b. They dislike the smell of rotting meat.
   c. They can weigh up to 11 kilograms each.
   d. They carry seeds to other areas of the forest.

5   What happens to flies according to paragraph 4?

   a. They eat the seeds of a corpse flower.
   b. They become covered in a flower's pollen.
   c. They produce a sweet-smelling scent.
   d. They carry flowers to a new location.

6   What insects are attracted to the Titan Arum?

Organizing the Passage

Complete the organizer with the words in the box.

Plants that Stink	
The Titan Arum	• can grow up to 3 meters tall • gets its name because it smells like ❶ _____ meat
The Stinking Corpse Lily	• can weigh up to 11 kilograms • attracts animals and ❷ _____ with its smell
The Dead ❸ _____ Arum Lily	• traps ❹ _____ inside its flowers • ❺ _____ the flies in pollen, then releases them

covers	flies	insects	rotting	horse

Summarizing the Passage

The following is a summary of the passage. Fill in the blanks with the appropriate words.

pollen	ensures	forest	attract	meat

Some plants produce disgusting smells that ❶ _____ insects. The Titan Arum is native to Indonesia. It smells similar to rotting ❷ _____. Beetles and flies are attracted to this smell. The Stinking Corpse Lily also grows in Indonesia. ❸ _____ animals are attracted to its rotting meat smell. Similarly, the Dead Horse Arum Lily smells like a dead horse. This flower traps flies and covers them in ❹ _____. The flies carry the pollen to other flowers, which ❺ _____ the plant survives.

Unit 10
Plant Growing Seasons

Think about the Topic

1 What happens to plants during the winter?

2 Which plants survive winter? How many years can they live for?

Vocabulary Preview

A   **Match the words with their definitions by writing the letter in each blank.**

1 life cycle _____ a. the main body of a plant

2 rare _____ b. a small tree or bush

3 period _____ c. the time from birth to death

4 single _____ d. an amount of time

5 root _____ e. a piece of a larger whole

6 stem _____ f. one

7 shrub _____ g. not commonly found

8 portion _____ h. the part of the plant that grows underground

B   **Choose the words that have similar** (sim.) **or opposite** (opp.) **meanings from the box.**

uncommon	specific	finish

1 rare _____ sim.

2 certain _____ sim.

3 complete (v.) _____ sim.

Background Knowledge

<u>The Life Cycle of Plants:</u>

1. Plants begin as a seed.
2. The seed grows into a young plant.
3. The young plant grows larger and matures.
4. Flowers bloom on the mature plant.
5. As the flowers wilt, fruits begin to grow.
6. Fruits carry seeds that will grow into new plants.

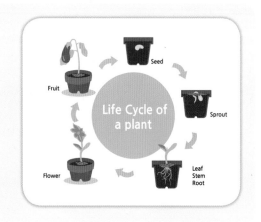

Plant Growing Seasons

Q

What is each paragraph mainly about?

P2 Plants with

_____

growing season

P3 Plants with

_____

growing seasons

All living things have their own unique **life cycle**. Some plants complete their life cycle in one or two growing seasons. But some **rare** species can live for several thousand years. There are three main life cycle classifications for plants: annual, biennial, and perennial.

5 Annuals usually begin life as a seed, undergo a growing **period**, and then produce their own seeds before dying. This happens over a very short time, often only a few weeks to a few months. Many common garden flowers are classified as annuals. Marigolds, for example, complete their life cycle in a **single** growing season. **❶**

10 Biennials, on the other hand, grow for two seasons. Onions and carrots are both biennials. They require up to two years to complete their entire life cycle. In the first year, they grow **roots**, **stems**, and leaves. They begin growing fruits and seeds in the second year. **❷** By the end of the second growing season, they begin to die.

❸ Plants that live for many years are called perennials. Typically, they produce seeds every year, but they do not die after. Trees and **shrubs**, for example, can live for many years. ❹ <u>Only certain **portions** of a perennial, such as the flowers and leaves, die in winter.</u> In summer, the plant's stems, flowers, and leaves tend to grow back.

Words 224

¹⁵ P4 Plants with (one / many) growing seasons

i **Trees:** Trees are some of the longest-living perennials. With proper nutrients and water, a tree can grow for thousands of years. The oldest living tree is estimated to be over 4,000 years old.

What is the passage mainly about?

a. How annuals compare to biennials
b. The oldest living plants on Earth
c. How plants grow during warm months
d. The three main life cycles of plants

Reading Comprehension

● **Answer the following questions.**

1   Which is true according to paragraph 1?

   a. Rare plant species can live for thousands of years.
   b. There are four main plant life cycle classifications.
   c. Annuals are the most common type of plant life cycle.
   d. Biennials are usually only found in warm regions.

2   Why does the author mention marigolds?

   a. To compare two life cycles
   b. To name a well-known perennial
   c. To list possible biennial plants
   d. To give an example of an annual

3   The word They in paragraph 3 refers to

   a. Stems   b. Biennials   c. Flowers   d. Annuals

4   What does the underlined part in the passage mean?

   a. Seeds are produced just before winter.
   b. Only flowers tend to die in cold weather.
   c. Leaves begin to grow back soon after winter.
   d. The entire perennial does not die in winter.

5   Where would the following sentence best fit in the passage?

Some flowers, such as daisies, are also perennials.

   a. ❶   b. ❷   c. ❸   d. ❹

6   What happens to a biennial at the end of its second growing season?

   _____

76

Organizing the Passage

Complete the organizer with the words in the box.

Plant Growing Seasons

Annuals	• They live for a few weeks to a few ❶ _____ before dying. • They complete their life cycle in a single growing ❷ _____ .
❸ _____	• They grow roots, stems, and ❹ _____ in the first year. • They begin growing fruit and seeds in the second year.
Perennials	• Some of them produce ❺ _____ every year. • They can live for many years.

season	leaves	biennials	months	seeds

Summarizing the Passage

Put the following sentences in order to make an appropriate summary. The first sentence is provided.

There are three classifications for plants: annual, biennial, and perennial.

_____ Biennials, on the other hand, grow for two seasons before they begin to die.

_____ Only part of a perennial dies in winter and then grows back in summer.

_____ Finally, plants that live for many years are classified as perennials.

_____ First, annuals live for a single growing season before they die.

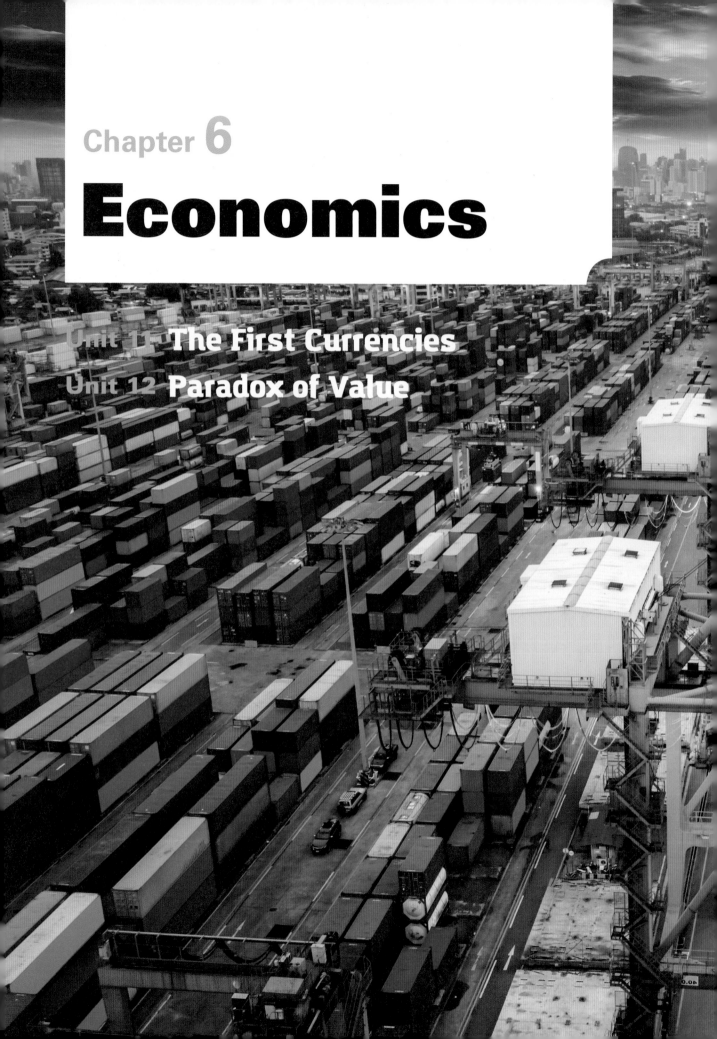

Chapter 6
Economics

Unit 11 The First Currencies
Unit 12 Paradox of Value

Economics is the study of how economies work. Economists examine how goods and services are produced and sold. They also study how goods and services are purchased and used by people and businesses.

Unit 11

The First Currencies

Think about the Topic

1   How do you normally pay for things?

2   What types of money are used these days?

Vocabulary Preview

A **Match the words with their definitions by writing the letter in each blank.**

1 weapon _____   a. to appear

2 barter _____   b. to trade goods or services without money

3 debt _____   c. to produce many of the same item

4 emerge _____   d. having a lot of worth

5 valuable _____   e. money owed

6 service _____   f. to make a fake copy of something

7 forge _____   g. a tool used to harm or defend

8 manufacture _____   h. work done for someone

B **Choose the words that have similar** *(sim.)* **or opposite** *(opp.)* **meanings from the box.**

defect	disappear	tough

1 emerge   _____ *opp.*

2 flaw   _____ *sim.*

3 difficult   _____ *sim.*

Background Knowledge

Modern Payment Methods:

Nowadays, people use many different types of money. Coins and paper bills are common. Credit cards are also a popular option when paying for items or services. Banking can also be done online. People can transfer funds via the Internet. They can also do their banking on their cell phones.

The First Currencies

Q

What is each paragraph mainly about?

P1 Early human (trade / money)

Before we had money, people got what they needed by trading. Food was traded for **weapons**. Fur was traded for **services**. People **bartered** when they traded. However, this system had many flaws. For example, it was difficult to keep track of **debts**. Eventually,
5 currency began to replace trade. These currencies looked much different from the money we use today.

P2 _____ as the first currency

The first currency was cattle. Animals were very important in early human societies. Cattle was used for transportation, food, and clothing. Thus, trading cattle became an important part of human
10 life. Naturally, values began to **emerge**. Cows were considered more **valuable** than goats. Sometimes a person could trade one cow for two or more goats.

▲ Traders bartering their wares

▲ Cowrie shells used in China

P3 Cowrie _____ as a currency

Around three thousand years ago, cowrie shells emerged as a currency. Cowrie shells were first used in China during the Shang
15 dynasty. Other regions, such as India and Africa, also began using them. Cowrie shells were traded for items and services. They were nearly impossible to **forge**, which made them an attractive option. Many other societies used these shells for hundreds of years.

▲ Old Chinese coins

In 1000 BC, there weren't enough cowrie shells. China began to **manufacture** their own. These shells were made from bronze and copper. Later, a flat version was made. These disks had holes in the center so they could be threaded onto a chain. Other societies also began using metals to make coins. Words 229

P4 The first (metal / shell) coins

20

▶ An ancient Greek gold coin

What is the passage mainly about?

a. Which types of cattle were traded
b. The discovery of cowrie shells
c. How currencies developed
d. China's first banks and money

i Coin Metals: Originally, copper, bronze, silver, and gold were used to make coins. Copper is still used today, but cheaper substances like zinc and nickel are more common.

Reading Comprehension

● **Answer the following questions.**

1 Why does the author mention fur in paragraph 1?

   a. To explain how cowrie shells were found

   b. To describe something that was traded

   c. To show how an item lost popularity

   d. To list something early humans ate

2 Which is NOT mentioned about cattle?

   a. Trading cattle was important to early humans.

   b. Animals were valued in early human societies.

   c. Cows were considered more valuable than goats.

   d. Two goats could be traded for three chickens.

3 The word them in the passage refers to

   a. societies   b. cattle   c. cowrie shells   d. regions

4 Which is closest in meaning to the word traded in paragraph 3?

   a. reversed   b. exchanged   c. discovered   d. returned

5 Why did China begin making metal cowrie shells?

   a. Too many people had begun forging the shells.

   b. Cattle had become more valuable than the shells.

   c. There weren't enough shells available at the time.

   d. Other regions were selling too many of the shells.

6 What was a flaw of the bartering system?

_____

Organizing the Passage

Complete the organizer with the words in the box.

The First Currencies	
Early Human Trade	• People bartered when they ❶ _____ . • This system had many flaws.
Cattle as the First Currency	• Cattle was used for ❷ _____ , food, and clothing. • Values began to emerge.
Cowrie Shells as a Currency	• The shells were traded for items and services. • They were a good option because they were nearly impossible to ❸ _____ .
The First Metal ❹ _____	• China made shells from bronze and copper in 1000 BC. • Later, a ❺ _____ version was made.

coins	forge	transportation	traded	flat

Summarizing the Passage

Put the following sentences in order to make an appropriate summary. The first sentence is provided.

> Before we had money, people got what they needed by trading.

_____   This system had many flaws, so currency began to replace trade.

_____   In 1000 BC, China began to make metal shells and later made a flat version.

_____   Around 3,000 years ago, cowrie shells emerged as an attractive currency option.

_____   As cattle was important in early human life, it became the first currency.

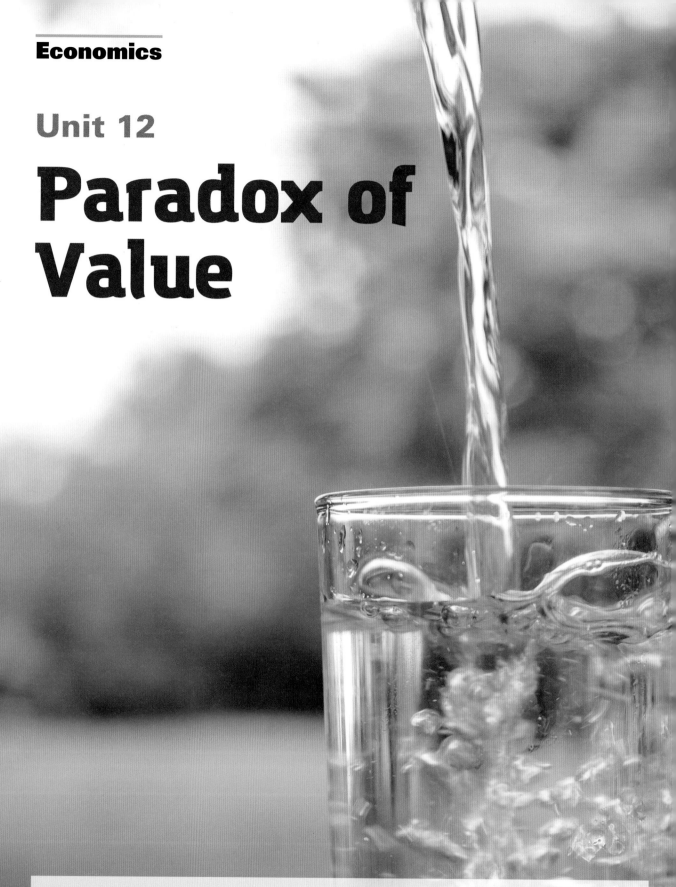

Unit 12

Paradox of Value

Think about the Topic

1 What do you need in order to survive?

2 What expensive item do you want? Do you need it to survive?

Vocabulary Preview

A   **Match the words with their definitions by writing the letter in each blank.**

1 essential _____ a. the need for fast action

2 logically _____ b. large in quantity

3 gem _____ c. in a way that shows clear reasoning

4 market price _____ d. necessary

5 abundant _____ e. to cause someone to get stuck somewhere

6 urgency _____ f. a stone with a high value

7 quality *(a.)* _____ g. of a high standard

8 strand *(v.)* _____ h. the amount paid for an item

B   **Choose the words that have similar** *(sim.)* **or opposite** *(opp.)* **meanings from the box.**

ready	unimportant	force

1 essential _____ *opp.*

2 willing _____ *sim.*

3 drive _____ *sim.*

Background Knowledge

The Five Basic Human Needs:

- Air: Oxygen is essential for breathing
- Fresh Water: Humans need to stay hydrated
- Food: Without quality food, humans will become sick or die
- Shelter: Humans need protection from harsh weather
- Sleep: Sleep recharges the body and mind

Paradox of Value

Many of Earth's resources are **essential** for human survival. Water, food, and clean air are just a few examples. **Logically**, these resources should be considered valuable. In reality, though, water is actually quite cheap. Rather, many non-essential resources are considered valuable.

⁵

What is each paragraph mainly about?

P2 The Paradox of

_____

This phenomenon is called the Paradox of Value, or the diamond-water paradox. Humans need water to survive, but we don't need precious **gems**. Since water is more useful, it should naturally have a higher **market price**. Diamonds, however, cost much more than
¹⁰ water. People will pay thousands of dollars for a single stone. The same is not true for a single glass of water.

P3 Why the paradox
(lowers / exists)

Why does this paradox exist? Earth has an **abundant** supply of water. Most people have steady access to clean water. This lowers the sense of **urgency** to find water. _____, the price
¹⁵ people are willing to pay for water also lowers. Diamonds, however, are rare. It is much more difficult to find **quality** diamonds. This fact drives the market price of diamonds up.

P4 How the paradox
(survives / reverses)

When water is in short supply, the
²⁰ diamond-water paradox often reverses. For example, a man may get **stranded** in a desert. He begins to die of thirst. A diamond will not save him. Water suddenly

becomes more valuable to him. This effect is temporary, however. Once survival is no longer an issue, the man will again pay more for diamonds. **Words 229**

25

 Precious Gems: Gems are crystals that are cut, polished, and used to make jewelry. Some gemstones are rare and valuable.

Check the main idea of the passage.

a. Humans sometimes do not value what they need.

b. Most of Earth's resources are gradually disappearing.

c. The Paradox of Value can easily be reversed.

d. The price of diamonds has lowered over the years.

Reading Comprehension

● **Answer the following questions.**

1 Which is true according to paragraph 1?

   a. Many non-essential items are expensive.

   b. Water is more useful for humans than air.

   c. Diamonds are more expensive than ever.

   d. Most resources are non-essential.

2 What does the underlined part of the passage mean?

   a. Most people prefer to buy water over diamonds.

   b. We need water much more than we need precious gems.

   c. People will not pay a high price for one glass of water.

   d. Water is in short supply, which has affected the cost.

3 What is the best choice for the blank?

   a. In conclusion   b. In turn   c. As with   d. As before

4 What can you guess about deserts?

   a. They are rich in resources.

   b. They do not have much water.

   c. It is common to get lost there.

   d. It is important to avoid them.

5 Why does the author mention a stranded man in paragraph 4?

   a. To explain the market price of gems

   b. To name the location of most diamonds

   c. To give an example of an essential resource

   d. To illustrate how the paradox reverses

6 What do most people have steady access to?

_____

Organizing the Passage

Complete the organizer with the words in the box.

Paradox of Value	
The Paradox of Value	• Humans need water to ❶ _____ , but water is cheap. • We don't need diamonds, but they are expensive.
Why the Paradox Exists	• Steady ❷ _____ lowers the sense of urgency to find water. • Diamonds are ❸ _____ , which drives the market price up.
How the Paradox ❹ _____	• A man stranded in a desert will begin to die of ❺ _____ . • Water suddenly becomes more valuable to him.

rare	access	survive	reverses	thirst

Summarizing the Passage

The following is a summary of the passage. Fill in the blanks with the appropriate words.

paradox	resources	diamonds	drives	urgency

Many non-essential ❶ _____ are considered valuable. This is called the Paradox of Value. Humans need water to survive. Naturally, it should have a higher price. However, gems like ❷ _____ cost much more. This occurs because people have steady access to clean water. This lowers the sense of ❸ _____ to find water. Diamonds, however, are rare. This ❹ _____ up the market price of diamonds. The diamond-water ❺ _____ can reverse. A man dying of thirst will value water much more than diamonds.

Chapter 7
Art

Art is an expression of human creativity. In its visual form, art can be sculpture or painting. However, art is always changing. Nowadays, artists even use technology to create digital artworks that can be printed or shared online.

Unit 13
John William Waterhouse

Think about the Topic

1 What is your favorite painting?

2 Who is your favorite artist?

Vocabulary Preview

A   **Match the words with their definitions by writing the letter in each blank.**

1 artistic _____   a. having skill in the arts

2 showcase _____   b. a person in a story

3 style _____   c. a way of doing something

4 inspire _____   d. having dream-like qualities

5 dreamy _____   e. a story explaining something about the ancient world

6 nature _____   f. the living world

7 character _____   g. to display

8 myth _____   h. to give ideas

B   **Choose the words that have similar (sim.) or opposite (opp.) meanings from the box.**

depart	vivid	tale

1 myth _____ sim.

2 return _____ opp.

3 bright _____ sim.

Background Knowledge

Raphael:

○ Full Name: Raffaello Sanzio da Urbino (1483-1520)

○ Focus: Sketches, paintings, frescos, architecture

○ Tools: Oil paint, glass, stone

○ Importance:

  • Painted figures with ideal beauty

  • Gave subjects more emotion

  • Changed the way people viewed art

John William Waterhouse

Q

What is each paragraph mainly about?

P1 Waterhouse's (birth / early life)

John William Waterhouse was an English painter. Born in 1849, Waterhouse grew up in an **artistic** family. His parents sent him to the Royal Academy of Art. Waterhouse studied classical art for many years. Many galleries **showcased** his work. His paintings became

5 very popular. But later, his **style** began to change.

P2 The pre-Raphaelite
_____

Waterhouse was **inspired** by the pre-Raphaelite Brotherhood. The Brotherhood was a group of seven artists. At the time, schools only taught classical art. ❶ This style was _____ the work of Raphael. But before Raphael, artists mostly painted nature. Their

10 work was **dreamy** and full of bright colors. ❷

P3 Waterhouse's (style / friendships)

Waterhouse was not a member of the Brotherhood. ❸ But he grew up during the movement. He started his career in the classical style. ❹ That changed over time, and he began to paint **nature**. His work started to feature fields, forests, and lakes. He used bright

15 colors and often included beautiful women. In many ways, his work looked like the Brotherhood's.

▲ *Ulysses and the Sirens* (1891)

▲ *Ophelia* (1894)

▲ *Dolce far Niente* (1880)

Waterhouse often painted **characters** from **myths**. He also painted scenes from literature. *Hamlet* was one of his favorites. Waterhouse especially enjoyed painting Ophelia. Usually, she is shown sitting by the water just before her death. Waterhouse's Ophelia paintings are his most famous. **Words 209**

20

P4 _____ in Waterhouse's work

ℹ *Hamlet's* Ophelia: *Hamlet* is one of Shakespeare's greatest tragedies. Ophelia, the female lead, drowns during the play. This character inspired many artists to recreate her death.

 Check the main idea of the passage.

a. Waterhouse was influenced by pre-Raphaelite art.

b. The pre-Raphaelite Brotherhood inspired many artists.

c. Hamlet is one of the most commonly painted characters.

d. Nature is featured in art more often than characters.

Reading Comprehension

● **Answer the following questions.**

1   What can you guess about Waterhouse's family?

    a. They were extremely wealthy.

    b. They encouraged his love of art.

    c. They attended the same art school.

    d. They were part of the Brotherhood.

2   Which is the best choice for the blank?

    a. explained as   b. offered from   c. requested for   d. based on

3   Which is NOT true about the Brotherhood?

    a. It was a group of seven artists.

    b. They used bright colors to paint.

    c. They rejected classical teachings.

    d. They admired Raphael's paintings.

4   Where would the following sentence best fit in the passage?

The Brotherhood wanted to return to this style.

    a. ❶   b. ❷   c. ❸   d. ❹

5   Which is true about Waterhouse's later work?

    a. It features bright colors and scenes from literature.

    b. It was showcased at the Royal Academy of Art.

    c. It depicts the seven members of the Brotherhood.

    d. It can be considered classical in style.

6   How did Waterhouse usually paint Ophelia?

Organizing the Passage

Complete the organizer with the words in the box.

Waterhouse's Early Life	• Waterhouse attended the Royal Academy of Art. • He studied ❶ _____ art for many years.
The Pre-Raphaelite Brotherhood	• It was a group of seven artists. • They wanted to ❷ _____ to a pre-Raphael style.
Waterhouse's Style	• He started in the classical ❸ _____. • Later, he began to paint nature and beautiful women.
❹ _____ in Waterhouse's Work	• Waterhouse often painted characters from ❺ _____. • He especially enjoyed painting Ophelia.

classical   literature   style   return   characters

Summarizing the Passage

The following is a summary of the passage. Fill in the blanks with the appropriate words.

older   nature   myths   painter   disliked

John William Waterhouse was a popular English ❶ _____. He studied classical art. However, his style changed over time. Waterhouse began to paint dreamy scenes of ❷ _____. He may have been inspired by the pre-Raphaelite Brotherhood. The Brotherhood ❸ _____ classical art. They wanted to return to an ❹ _____ style. Waterhouse also painted scenes from ❺ _____ and literature. He especially enjoyed painting Ophelia.

Unit 13   99

Unit 14
Japan's Digital Art Gallery

Think about the Topic

1   What is digital art?

2   Have you visited a digital art gallery?

Vocabulary Preview

A **Match the words with their definitions by writing the letter in each blank.**

1 bind _____ a. a type of lamp

2 social media _____ b. long-term

3 digital _____ c. a machine that shines light and images

4 permanent _____ d. websites used to socialize

5 projector _____ e. involving the use of computers

6 wander _____ f. to restrict

7 feature _____ g. to show something as an important part

8 lantern _____ h. to move without a destination

B **Choose the words that have similar** (*sim.*) **or opposite** (*opp.*) **meanings from the box.**

limit	guest	boring

1 bind _____ *sim.*

2 exciting _____ *opp.*

3 visitor _____ *sim.*

Background Knowledge

Types of Digital Art:

○ Photopainting: Artists use paint software to alter photos

○ Digital Collage: Artists combine and layer images with editing
    software

○ Digital Painting: Images are created entirely using paint software

○ Algorithmic: Math calculations are used to make computer-generated images

Japan's Digital Art Gallery

Q

What is each paragraph mainly about?

P1 How _____
changed art

P2 Who _____
Japan's digital art gallery

P3 How the gallery
(works / wanders)

As technology changes, so does art. Artists are not **bound** by traditional art mediums. Now, they can create digital art. They can share their work on **social media** or sell it online. Technology also affects how art is displayed. Art galleries are becoming more exciting
5 with computers.

One gallery has taken **digital** art to the next level. The Mori Building Digital Art Museum is located in Tokyo. The gallery was founded by a group called teamLab. Originally, teamLab traveled around the world. They held art shows in various cities. In 2018, they set up a
10 **permanent** space. They called the gallery teamLab Borderless.

TeamLab Borderless is unlike any gallery in the world. The building is large and has many rooms. There are hundreds of computers and **projectors** inside. These shine images on floors, walls, and ceilings. There are no tour guides or paths to follow. Visitors are free to

▼ *The Way of the Sea in the Crystal World* & *Ever-Changing* ©Tatiana SP & teamLab

▲ *Forest of Resonating Lamps* © teamLab

wander. They can spend as much time as they like in their favorite
scenes. ¹⁵

Many of the rooms **feature** images of nature. Some rooms are full
of mirrors and lights. Others have thousands of glowing **lanterns**. The
scenes are always changing. This means each visitor has a unique
experience. They are encouraged to take many photographs. Then ²⁰
they can share them on social media. The art is always moving, so no
two photographs are ever the same. **Words 226**

P4 What _____
experience

i **The First Digital Art:**
John Whitney is
considered one of the
fathers of computer
graphics. In the 1960s,
he used early computer
technology to create
artwork.

 What is the passage mainly about?

　　a. How to buy and sell digital art
　　b. A new type of art gallery in Japan
　　c. Computer technology and social media
　　d. The best place to set up an art gallery

Reading Comprehension

● **Answer the following questions.**

1 Which is NOT mentioned as a way technology affects art?

    a. Computers make galleries more exciting.

    b. Artists can create digital art with technology.

    c. Works of art can be made quickly and more easily.

    d. Art can be shared and sold on the Internet.

2 Which is closest in meaning to the word Originally in paragraph 2?

    a. Initially   b. Lastly   c. Slightly   d. Surely

3 How is art displayed in the gallery?

    a. Visitors create their own digital images.

    b. Projectors shine images into the rooms.

    c. Real lanterns float through the space.

    d. Colorful photographs cover the walls.

4 Which is mentioned about visitors in paragraph 3?

    a. They are usually active on social media.

    b. They gave the gallery its unique name.

    c. They should not touch the computers.

    d. They don't need to follow a tour guide.

5 The word Others in paragraph 4 refers to

    a. Mirrors   b. Lights   c. Images   d. Rooms

6 What are visitors encouraged to do in teamLab Borderless?

_____

Organizing the Passage

Complete the organizer with the words in the box.

Japan's Digital Art Gallery	
How Technology Changed Art	• Artists can share and sell their work online. • Art galleries are becoming more exciting with computers.
Who ❶ _____ Japan's Digital Art Gallery	• The gallery was founded by teamLab. • They called the ❷ _____ teamLab Borderless.
How the Gallery Works	• There are hundreds of computers and ❸ _____ inside. • They shine images on floors, walls, and ceilings.
What Visitors Experience	• The rooms feature lights, mirrors, and ❹ _____ lanterns. • Visitors take ❺ _____ and share them on social media.

gallery	glowing	photographs	founded	projectors

Summarizing the Passage

Put the following sentences in order to make an appropriate summary. The first sentence is provided.

Art galleries are becoming more exciting with technology.

_____ The scenes are always changing, so each visitor has a unique experience.

_____ They shine images on the floors, walls, and ceilings of the rooms.

_____ A group called teamLab founded a digital art gallery in Tokyo.

_____ There are hundreds of computers and projectors inside.

Chapter 8
Psychology

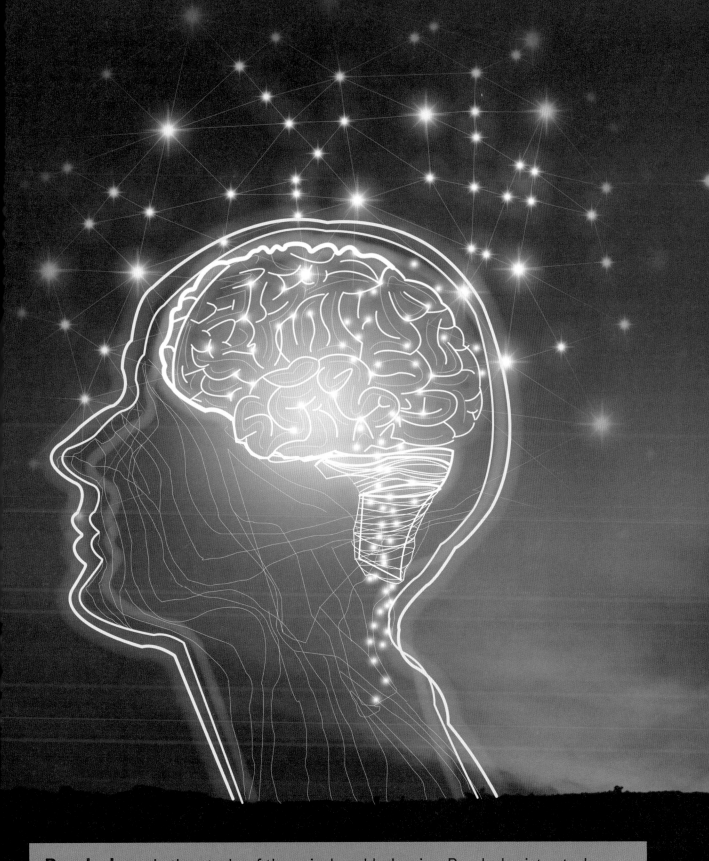

Psychology is the study of the mind and behavior. Psychologists study thought processes in humans or animals. They try to explain why a person or animal thinks, feels, or acts a certain way.

Unit 15

Emotional Support Animals

Think about the Topic

1   How do you feel when something bad happens?

2   How do you deal with bad feelings?

Vocabulary Preview

A   **Match the words with their definitions by writing the letter in each blank.**

1 cope with _____   a. to respond

2 trauma _____   b. mental harm caused by a bad situation

3 disorder _____   c. to act

4 reliable _____   d. to form a relationship

5 bond (v.) _____   e. a physical or mental condition that is not healthy

6 affectionate _____   f. showing a lot of love

7 behave _____   g. able to be trusted

8 react _____   h. to deal with

B   **Choose the words that have similar** (sim.) **or opposite** (opp.) **meanings from the box.**

distant	upset	severe

1 serious _____ sim.

2 calm _____ opp.

3 loving _____ opp.

Background Knowledge

Types of Therapy:

   When dealing with a difficult situation, some people get help from a trained therapist. Talking about a problem helps many people. Sometimes, though, therapy is not enough. Some people need constant comfort. Therapy animals are becoming a popular option.

Emotional Support Animals

Life is full of traumatic events. Many people experience accidents and deaths in the family. They might also be living with a serious illness. These events can harm a person's mental
5 health. Sometimes, they need therapy. This helps them **cope with** their feelings. These days, some people are turning to animals in their time of need.

Q

What is each paragraph mainly about?

P2 Why people (experience / need) support animals

10 People living with **trauma** may have a hard time making friends. ❶ They tend to get very lonely. ❷ Emotional support animals can help these people. Animals can offer friendship and comfort.
15 Similarly, a person with a mental **disorder** may have trouble dealing with stress. ❸ They might have a hard time calming down. ❹

P3 Types of _____ animals

Dogs tend to make the best support animals. There are a few reasons for this. Dogs are **reliable** and **bond** well with humans. Cats can also make good support animals. Some cats are as playful
20 and **affectionate** as dogs. Many cats have become support animals in recent years. Sometimes, even miniature horses are chosen. Rodents and birds may also become support animals.

P4 What makes a (good / bad) support animal

Unlike most working animals, support animals don't need special training. The animals **behave** like regular pets. However, not all pets

make good support animals. It depends on the pet's personality. The ²⁵ animal must be very loving. It must also be sensitive to an owner's feelings. It should know how to **react** to these feelings.   Words 230

 PTSD: PTSD, or post-traumatic stress disorder, is a mental disorder caused by a stressful or traumatic event. People with PTSD may experience flashbacks, nightmares, and anxiety.

💡 **Check the main idea of the passage.**

a. Training support animals can be helpful.

b. Rodents make the best support animals.

c. Dogs do not always respond to training.

d. Animals can help people deal with trauma.

Reading Comprehension

● **Answer the following questions.**

1   Which is closest in meaning to the word events in paragraph 1?

    a. explanations   b. procedures   c. situations   d. guesses

2   Where would the following sentence best fit in the passage?

Support animals can help them stay calm.

    a. ❶   b. ❷   c. ❸   d. ❹

3   What does the underlined part of the passage mean?

    a. Cats and dogs may have similar personalities.

    b. Cats are more loving than dogs are.

    c. Dogs are the most affectionate animals.

    d. Both cats and dogs are good pets for kids.

4   What is mentioned about miniature horses?

    a. They live longer than dogs and cats.

    b. They bond well with rodents and birds.

    c. They need training to become support animals.

    d. They sometimes become support animals.

5   Which is NOT true according to paragraph 4?

    a. Some pets aren't good support animals.

    b. Support animals should be very loving.

    c. Some people react badly to support animals.

    d. Support animals must be sensitive pets.

6   Why do dogs make the best support animals?

Organizing the Passage

Complete the organizer with the words in the box.

Emotional Support Animals

Why People Need Support Animals	• People with ❶ _____ have a hard time making friends. • They may have trouble dealing with ❷ _____ .
Types of Support Animals	• Dogs and cats are ❸ _____ and affectionate support animals. • Horses, ❹ _____ , and birds can also be support animals.
What Makes a Good Support Animal	• The animal must be very loving. • It must be ❺ _____ to an owner's feelings.

sensitive   playful   trauma   stress   rodents

Summarizing the Passage

The following is a summary of the passage. Fill in the blanks with the appropriate words.

support   training   health   birds   offer

Certain events can harm a person's mental ❶ _____ . These days, people are turning to animals to cope with their feelings. Emotional support animals can ❷ _____ friendship and comfort. Dogs tend to make the best ❸ _____ animals. However, many cats have also become support animals in recent years. Sometimes, horses, rodents, and ❹ _____ are also chosen. Support animals don't need any special ❺ _____ . But the animal must be very loving and sensitive to an owner's feelings.

Unit 16
Phobias

Think about the Topic

1 What are you most afraid of?

2 What are some common phobias?

Vocabulary Preview

A   **Match the words with their definitions by writing the letter in each blank.**

1 fear   _____   a. to become stronger

2 intensify   _____   b. very fast

3 excessive   _____   c. to tell

4 open space   _____   d. a physical reaction

5 symptom   _____   e. a tool used to give an injection

6 rapid   _____   f. too much

7 report (v.)   _____   g. a large area without walls

8 needle   _____   h. something a person is afraid of; to feel afraid

B   **Choose the words that have similar** (sim.) **or opposite** (opp.) **meanings from the box.**

slow	bad	better

1 unpleasant   _____ *sim.*

2 rapid   _____ *opp.*

3 worse   _____ *opp.*

Background Knowledge

Common Phobias:

○ Arachnophobia: Fear of spiders

○ Hemophobia: Fear of blood or bleeding

○ Agoraphobia: Fear of a situation, such as being in an open space

○ Astraphobia: Fear of thunder and lightning during storms

○ Aviophobia: Fear of flying or being in an airplane

Phobias

Q

What is each paragraph mainly about?

P1 Normal _____

P2 What a _____
is

P3 _____ of
phobias

Having **fears** is a normal part of life. As children, many people fear spiders or ghosts. They might grow out of these fears as they age. However, their fears may **intensify** over time. When faced with a fear, some people have an extreme reaction. They may actually be
5 suffering from a phobia.

Phobias cause an **excessive** amount of fear. This fear can relate to an object or a situation. For example, some people have a spider phobia. If they see a spider, they will experience an extreme reaction. The same is true for a person who has a phobia of **open spaces**. If
10 they enter an open space, they will experience a negative reaction.

There are many **symptoms** associated with phobias. Some people may shake or feel sick to their stomach. They might also sweat or have a **rapid** heartbeat. These symptoms may cause the phobia to get worse. This happens because the symptoms are almost always
15 unpleasant. The sufferer will begin to fear the symptoms, too.

The most common phobias involve nature. Many people **report** insect and snake phobias. Some even fear natural events, such as storms. Health care is another common cause of phobias. A fear of **needles** or blood can stop someone from visiting a hospital. Finally, many everyday situations can ²⁰ cause phobias. For example, fear of flying can make traveling very hard. These phobias make life more difficult. **Words 232**

P4 (Common / Visiting) phobias

What is the passage mainly about?

a. Treatments for common phobias

b. How fears change over time

c. The fear of snakes and insects

d. Phobias and associated symptoms

i Treatment of Phobias: Many people with phobias undergo therapy as a treatment. However, some medications may be given to reduce the symptoms of panic.

Reading Comprehension

- **Answer the following questions.**

1 **What happens to children according to paragraph 1?**

   a. They might lose their fears.

   b. They develop new fears.

   c. Their fear of ghosts grows.

   d. They start to fear open spaces.

2 **Which is NOT true according to paragraph 2?**

   a. Some people have a spider phobia.

   b. Phobias can cause extreme reactions.

   c. Phobias relate to objects and situations.

   d. Fear of open spaces is a rare phobia.

3 **Which is closest in meaning to the word shake in paragraph 3?**

   a. shove   b. tremble   c. resist   d. wail

4 **Which is true according to paragraph 3?**

   a. Phobias may get worse over time.

   b. Not all symptoms are unpleasant.

   c. Having a rapid heartbeat is dangerous.

   d. Medication can prevent sweating.

5 **Why does the author mention a fear of needles or blood in paragraph 4?**

   a. To mention why injections are given

   b. To list the effects of a phobia on the body

   c. To describe how to overcome a phobia

   d. To give an example of a health care phobia

6 **What can fear of flying do?**

_____

Organizing the Passage

Complete the organizer with the words in the box.

	Phobias
Normal Fears	• Many children fear spiders or ghosts. • They might grow out of these fears or the fears could intensify.
What a Phobia Is	• A phobia is an excessive amount of ❶ _____. • It can relate to an ❷ _____ or situation.
❸ _____ of Phobias	• People may shake or feel sick to their stomach. • They might also have a rapid ❹ _____.
Common Phobias	• Many people report insect or snake phobias. • Some fear storms, health care, and even ❺ _____.

flying	fear	symptoms	object	heartbeat

Summarizing the Passage

Put the following sentences in order to make an appropriate summary. The first sentence is provided.

Fears are normal, but some people may be suffering from a phobia.

_____ When faced with the object or situation, people have an extreme reaction.

_____ These symptoms are unpleasant and may cause the phobia to get worse.

_____ Phobias cause an excessive amount of fear about a situation or object.

_____ As a result, many common phobias make life more difficult.

TOEFL
Practice Test

TOEFL Practice Test ❶

The First Woman in Space

Valentina Tereshkova loved to fly. Born in 1937, Tereshkova grew up in the Soviet Union. She became a textile worker, but her greatest joy was skydiving. In the 1960s, Tereshkova got her chance to fly where no woman had ever gone: space.

The infamous Space Race began in the 1950s. The United States and the Soviet Union competed for many years. Both countries wanted to be the first to send pilots into space. They also wanted to send an astronaut to the moon. NASA had plans to send a female pilot to space. Soon, the Soviet space program formed its own all-female pilot team.

Tereshkova's skydiving experience got her a place in the Soviet program. Her team went through months of intense training. Then Tereshkova was chosen to pilot the Vostok 6. In 1963, she made history. She was only 26, but she became the first woman to go to space. Tereshkova spent nearly three days in orbit. During that time, she traveled around Earth 48 times.

The flight changed Tereshkova's life. She became an inspiration to many women. It also launched her political career. Leaders all over the world invited Tereshkova to visit their countries. Later, she was chosen for several political positions. She was even invited to carry the Olympic torch in 2008 and 2014.

1   **According to the passage, which of the following is true about Tereshkova?**

   Ⓐ She went to space in the 1960s.

   Ⓑ She was born in the United States.

   Ⓒ She took a job as a pilot at NASA.

   Ⓓ She worked as a skydiving instructor.

2   **The word "competed" in the passage is closest in meaning to**

   Ⓐ launched

   Ⓑ trained

   Ⓒ fought

   Ⓓ requested

3 **According to paragraph 3, Tereshkova got a place in the Soviet program because**

(A) she wanted to join NASA eventually

(B) she had been to space in the Vostok 6

(C) she knew the job of a textile worker

(D) she had experience as a skydiver

4 **According to paragraph 3, which is NOT true about Tereshkova's flight?**

(A) It took nearly three days to complete.

(B) It required 26 months of intense training.

(C) It involved 48 orbits around Earth.

(D) It was the first space flight taken by a woman.

5 **Which of the following can be inferred from paragraph 4 about Tereshkova?**

(A) She preferred life as an astronaut.

(B) She was admired internationally.

(C) She hoped to compete in the Olympics.

(D) She moved to another country.

6 **An introductory sentence for a brief summary of the passage is provided below. Complete the summary by selecting the THREE answer choices that express the most important ideas of the passage. Some sentences do not belong because they express ideas that are not presented in the passage or are minor ideas in the passage.**

In the 1950s, the United States and the Soviet Union competed in the Space Race.

❶ Tereshkova was chosen for the team and piloted the Vostok 6.

❷ Tereshkova carried the Olympic torch in both 2008 and 2014.

❸ After, Tereshkova inspired many people and became a politician.

❹ The team was men and women who trained over several months.

❺ The Soviet Union formed an all-female team to compete with NASA.

TOEFL Practice Test ❷

Homeschooling

Long ago, most parents taught their children at home. There were not many schoolhouses and most children did not live close to one. Over time, public schools became standard. Laws were made to ensure children went to school. However, this has changed over the last few decades. Some parents have begun teaching their children at home.

Homeschooling is the practice of educating children at home. One or both parents handle the educational needs of the children. Occasionally, parents hire a tutor to act as the teacher. Since the early 2000s, more and more parents around the world have chosen homeschooling. However, the practice is still not legal in some countries, such as Greece and Brazil where children must attend school regularly.

Homeschooling is an attractive option for many reasons. School learning can be very rigid. Some students may not thrive in that environment. At home, they can study at their own pace. They can focus on the subjects they enjoy most. Additionally, studying at home keeps kids out of trouble. They are no longer negatively influenced by their peers.

There are a few downsides of homeschooling, too. Teaching children at home takes a lot of time and effort. One parent may have to give up his or her job. This can cause financial trouble for the family. Additionally, children learn how to socialize at school. They will not be able to learn these skills if they study at home.

---

1 **According to paragraph 1, which is NOT true about education long ago?**

  Ⓐ Most parents taught children at home.

  Ⓑ There were laws against homeschooling.

  Ⓒ There were not many schoolhouses.

  Ⓓ Most children lived far from schools.

2 **Which of the sentences below best expresses the essential information in the highlighted sentence in the passage? Incorrect answer choices change the meaning in important ways or leave out essential information.**

  However, the practice is still not legal in some countries, such as Greece and Brazil where children must attend school regularly.

(A) Brazil and Greece are the only countries that haven't legalized homeschooling.

(B) Brazil and Greece were among the first nations to stop homeschooling.

(C) In some countries like Brazil and Greece, children can't legally be homeschooled.

(D) Unlike Greece and Brazil, most countries allow children to study at home.

3 **The word "thrive" in the passage is closest in meaning to**

(A) influence   (B) cover

(C) succeed   (D) create

4 **Why does the author mention "financial trouble" in paragraph 4?**

(A) To name a negative factor of homeschooling

(B) To list a reason why homeschooling is attractive

(C) To compare homeschooling in two countries

(D) To disprove a common opinion about education

5 **The word "They" in the passage refers to**

(A) Parents   (B) Countries

(C) Downsides   (D) Children

6 **An introductory sentence for a brief summary of the passage is provided below. Complete the summary by selecting the THREE answer choices that express the most important ideas of the passage. Some sentences do not belong because they express ideas that are not presented in the passage or are minor ideas in the passage.**

> Over the past few decades, parents have begun educating their children at home again.

1. Parents may have to give up working to teach the children.
2. There are many benefits, such as keeping kids out of trouble.
3. Homeschooling is the practice of educating a child at home.
4. Children tend to focus better in a quiet classroom environment.
5. However, homeschooling can cause financial and socializing problems.

Glaciers

Glaciers make up around 10 percent of Earth's surface. Nearly all of Earth's glacial ice can be found in the polar regions. For example, glacier ice covers about 98 percent of Antarctica. However, glaciers can also be seen on some mountains, such as the Andes and the Himalayas. How do glaciers form and move?

Over thousands of years, ice and snow gather to form glaciers. Glaciers become so heavy that they begin to move. On average, they move about 1 meter per day. **1** However, this speed varies. **2** Some glaciers go through periods of inactivity and do not move at all. **3** When they move, they change the landscape. **4**

Some glaciers go through seasonal changes. They gather ice and snow during colder seasons. But in warmer seasons, some of the ice melts. This meltwater is important for nearby wildlife. Plants and animals rely on it to survive the warm summer months. Climate change also affects glaciers by increasing the amount of meltwater. Scientists often study glaciers to determine the rate of global warming.

Glacier ice looks much different from regular ice. Regular ice is often white or clear. But glaciers have a distinctive blue color. This occurs because glacier ice is compressed. There are very few air bubbles in the ice. Air bubbles give regular ice its white color while compressed ice appears blue.

1   **According to paragraph 1, which is NOT true about glacial ice?**

Ⓐ It makes up 98 percent of Antarctica.

Ⓑ It forms during rainy seasons.

Ⓒ Most of it is in the polar regions.

Ⓓ It covers about 10 percent of Earth.

2   **According to paragraph 2, glaciers move because**

Ⓐ they gather snow

Ⓑ they melt in summer

Ⓒ they are made of ice

Ⓓ they are so heavy

3 **Which of the following can be inferred from paragraph 3 about plants and animals?**

Ⓐ They follow glaciers as they move.

Ⓑ They consume glacier meltwater.

Ⓒ They live in valleys made by glaciers.

Ⓓ They add bubbles to glacier ice.

4 **According to paragraph 4, why do glaciers appear blue?**

Ⓐ There are air bubbles in the ice.

Ⓑ The ice has been compressed.

Ⓒ Sunlight reflects on the glacier.

Ⓓ Water has a natural blue color.

5 **Look at the four squares [■] that indicate where the following sentence could be added to the passage.**

They may leave behind valleys, crevices, and even lakes.

Where would the sentence best fit?

6 **An introductory sentence for a brief summary of the passage is provided below. Complete the summary by selecting the THREE answer choices that express the most important ideas of the passage. Some sentences do not belong because they express ideas that are not presented in the passage or are minor ideas in the passage.**

Glaciers are moving areas of ice that make up 10 percent of Earth's surface.

❶ Glacial ice grows so heavy that it moves, changing the landscape.

❷ Air bubbles gather together to give the ice its distinctive white color.

❸ Over thousands of years, ice and snow form heavy glaciers.

❹ In summer, glaciers move continuously over the land, forming lakes.

❺ Glaciers go through seasonal changes and are affected by climate change.

TOEFL Practice Test ④

The Silk Road

The Silk Road was an important early trade route. It began in the 2nd century BCE. For centuries, it grew, connecting the East with the West. Eventually, a network of routes formed. Goods were carried across entire continents. However, people traded more than goods. The Silk Road was also a place to trade culture and religion.

The Silk Road stretched across three continents: Asia, Africa, and Europe. It got its name from silk, as silk was one of the most highly traded items. However, travelers sold many other goods. Spices, nuts, and porcelain were just a few. Relay trade was common at the time. This meant goods passed from trader to trader. Eventually, they made their way to a buyer.

The Silk Road affected more than just business. Travelers spread philosophy and religion. Science, technology, and art also spread this way. Over time, towns developed along the routes. These towns turned into large cities. This changed the shape of the land. Cultures grew as people lived and worked together.

There was one negative consequence of the Silk Road. It affected the spread of disease. Some traders carried parasites. Archaeologists have found evidence of this. Unsanitary conditions at trade stops may have contributed. Other deadly diseases, such as *bubonic plague and *leprosy, may have also traveled the Silk Road.

*bubonic plague: Bubonic plague is a deadly disease caused by bacteria. It's estimated to have killed up to 200 million people in Europe and Asia during the 1300s.
*leprosy: Leprosy is a disease that affects the skin and nerves. Untreated, it can cause severe deformities and even death.

---

1 **The word "entire" in the passage is closest in meaning to**

 Ⓐ whole   Ⓑ important

 Ⓒ enormous   Ⓓ vibrant

2 **The word "they" in the passage refers to**

 Ⓐ continents   Ⓑ travelers

 Ⓒ goods   Ⓓ spices

3   According to paragraph 3, which is NOT true about the Silk Road?

    (A) Spices and nuts were produced close by.

    (B) Science, art, and technology spread there.

    (C) Cities and cultures developed nearby.

    (D) Philosophy and religion were traded there.

4   According to paragraph 4, parasites may have spread because

    (A) people ate unclean food

    (B) trade stops were unsanitary

    (C) the weather was too hot

    (D) nuts were infected

5   Why does the author mention "bubonic plague and leprosy"?

    (A) To mention a side-effect of spreading religion

    (B) To express the seriousness of the diseases exchanged

    (C) To explain how diseases passed between people

    (D) To describe how the Silk Road lost popularity

6   An introductory sentence for a brief summary of the passage is provided below. Complete the summary by selecting the THREE answer choices that express the most important ideas of the passage. Some sentences do not belong because they express ideas that are not presented in the passage or are minor ideas in the passage.

> The Silk Road was an important trade route that grew for centuries.

   1 The spread of diseases was a major negative effect of the Silk Road.

   2 Archeologists have found evidence that many traders had parasites.

   3 Relay trade became a common practice after the 15th century BCE.

   4 The route got its name from silk, but many other goods were traded there.

   5 Cities grew along the Silk Road where philosophy, art, and science spread.

MEMO

MEMO

MEMO

Building Background Knowledge for Academic Subjects

Fundamental Reading

Rachel Somer

Workbook

BASIC **1**

DARAKWON

Building Background Knowledge for Academic Subjects

Fundamental Reading

Rachel Somer

Workbook

BASIC 1

DARAKWON

Unit 1 The Fiery Crater

Vocabulary

A **Match the words with their correct meanings.**

a pocket of	endanger	assume	crater	gateway

1 an entrance into an area _____

2 to make a guess _____

3 to put in danger _____

4 a small area containing something _____

5 a large hole in a planet's surface _____

B **Choose the words from the box to complete the sentences.**

craters	store	collapsed	wonder

1 Some workers were injured when the ground _____.

2 The Grand Canyon is a geological _____ in the United States.

3 They discovered a large _____ of diamonds in the cave.

4 The moon's surface is covered in large _____.

Translation

C **Read the sentences and translate them into your language.**

1 Surprisingly, this crater has been on fire since the 1970s.

  → _____

2 The oil company worried the escaping gases would reach those villages.

  → _____

3 Local people call the crater the Door to Hell because it appears to be a fiery gateway into Earth.

  → _____

2

Paraphrasing

D **Paraphrase the sentences from the passage with the words in the box.**

keep them safe	found in	assumed
previously	biggest	set

1 Located in Turkmenistan, the crater is one of the largest natural gas stores on Earth.

→ _____ Turkmenistan, the crater is one of Earth's _____ natural gas pockets.

2 Oil drillers once thought the Karakum Desert was an oil field.

→ Oil drillers _____ believed the Karakum Desert to be an oil field.

3 The best way to protect them was to burn the gas, so geologists lit the crater on fire.

→ The best way to _____ was to burn the gas, so geologists _____ the crater ablaze.

4 It contains more natural gas than anyone first thought.

→ It holds more natural gas than anyone _____.

Listening

E **Listen to the summary and fill in the blanks.**

In 1971, oil drillers found a ❶ _____ of natural gas in the Karakum Desert. The ground suddenly ❷ _____ and formed a huge crater. The oil company worried escaping gases would hurt the ❸ _____. Geologists ❹ _____ to burn the gas, so they lit the crater on fire. The crater has been on fire ever since because it contains so much ❺ _____ gas. Locals call the crater the Door to Hell. Tourists travel to the Karakum Desert just to see the ❻ _____ crater.

Unit 2 Geothermal Energy

Vocabulary

A **Match the words with their correct meanings.**

absorb	pump	turbine	remaining	rely on

1 a machine that spins _____

2 to pull into _____

3 to need for comfort or survival _____

4 to push a liquid through a pipe _____

5 leftover _____

B **Choose the words from the box to complete the sentences.**

cools	buried	pipes	rely on

1 The _____ carry clean water to the house.

2 The cave environment _____ the air in summer.

3 The turbine was _____ deep beneath the building.

4 What resources do humans _____ most?

Translation

C **Read the sentences and translate them into your language.**

1 Geothermal energy is one of the cleanest resources on the planet.

➡ _____

2 A geothermal system can cool a home during warmer months.

➡ _____

3 Geothermal power plants are especially beneficial because they don't harm the environment.

➡ _____

Paraphrasing

D **Paraphrase the sentences from the passage with the words in the box.**

rotates	sources	run
warmth	remains	generates

1 People rely on many types of energy to heat and power their homes.

→ People use many _____ of energy to heat and _____ their homes.

2 The temperature underground stays the same all year long.

→ The temperature beneath the ground _____ the same the entire year.

3 The heat is used to warm the air of the home.

→ The _____ is used to warm up the air inside the home.

4 The heat from the steam spins a turbine, which makes electricity.

→ The heat of the vapor _____ a turbine, which _____ electricity.

Listening

E **Listen to the summary and fill in the blanks.**

Geothermal energy is a clean resource that is found ❶ _____. It can be used in a few ways. Geothermal heating systems use ❷ _____ buried underground. A liquid absorbs heat and then ❸ _____ back into a home. There, it warms the air. This system can also ❹ _____ a home in warmer months. Instead, it carries the heat back underground. ❺ _____ power plants can make ❻ _____ by using steam to spin a turbine. This electricity travels to homes.

Unit 3 The Red Panda

Vocabulary

A **Match the words with their correct meanings.**

habitat	related to	unique	poaching	herbivore

1 the act of killing endangered species _____

2 the place an animal lives _____

3 special _____

4 being in the same family with someone _____

5 an animal that eats only plants _____

B **Choose the words from the box to complete the sentences.**

active	native to	markings	herbivores

1 Each zebra has its own special pattern of _____.

2 Lions and giraffes are _____ the plains of Africa.

3 Rabbits are considered _____ since they don't eat meat.

4 Bats tend to be _____ only at night and rest during the day.

Translation

C **Read the sentences and translate them into your language.**

1 Unlike the name suggests, red pandas aren't closely related to giant pandas.

➜ _____

2 They prefer forested areas where they can climb and sleep in trees.

➜ _____

3 There are fewer than 10,000 red pandas living in the wild.

➜ _____

Paraphrasing

D Paraphrase the sentences from the passage with the words in the box.

resemble	patterns	regions
resting	homes	typically

1 The markings on their faces and tails are similar to raccoons.

→ The _____ on their faces and tails _____ raccoons.

2 Red pandas are known for lazily relaxing on tree branches during the day.

→ Red pandas are famous for lazily _____ on tree branches in the daytime.

3 This is mostly due to the destruction of their habitat.

→ This is _____ because of the destruction of their _____.

4 In these areas, poaching is illegal.

→ In these _____, poaching is against the law.

Listening

E Listen to the summary and fill in the blanks.

Red pandas are not members of the giant panda or raccoon ❶ _____. Their unique appearance puts them in their own family. ❷ _____ to the Himalayas and China, red pandas prefer ❸ _____ areas. They relax during the day but become ❹ _____ at night. There are fewer than 10,000 red pandas alive. This is due to the destruction of their habitat as well as ❺ _____. Also, birth rates are very low for red pandas. India and China have made protected areas for them. However, poaching still ❻ _____.

Unit 4 **Crow Intelligence**

Vocabulary

A   **Match the words with their correct meanings.**

reputation	compete	respond	swoop	socialize

1   to interact with others   _____

2   to attempt to beat someone at something   _____

3   the opinions held about someone or something   _____

4   to move downward very quickly   _____

5   to react to someone or something   _____

B   **Choose the words from the box to complete the sentences.**

encounter	memories	aggression	socialize

1   Elephants are very clever animals with excellent _____.

2   He was terrified after his _____ with a snake.

3   Tigers do not like to _____ with other animals.

4   Gorillas may show _____ when they feel threatened.

Translation

C   **Read the sentences and translate them into your language.**

1   She was certain these birds were thanking her for feeding them.

     ➔ _____

2   Scientists believe crows owe their intelligence to their brain size.

     ➔ _____

3   They compete with other members of the group as they look for a mate.

     ➔ _____

Paraphrasing

D **Paraphrase the sentences from the passage with the words in the box.**

| a result of | destructively | got larger |
| passed | operate | intelligent |

1 Over the years, Gabi's collection of gifts grew.

→ As the years _____, Gabi's collection of presents _____.

2 Some species of crow are even clever enough to use tools.

→ Some types of crow are even _____ enough to _____ tools.

3 This may be due to the way they socialize with each other

→ This may be _____ how they socialize with others.

4 They may respond negatively when a human is unkind or violent.

→ They might respond _____ when a person is mean or aggressive.

Listening

E **Listen to the summary and fill in the blanks.**

   Crows have a reputation for being very ❶ _____. Scientists think this is because of their ❷ _____ size. The brain of a crow is quite large compared to its body. This intelligence helps them use simple ❸ _____. Crows are also known for having very good memories. They ❹ _____ how they compete with other crows in their ❺ _____. Crows will also remember the kindness and aggression of ❻ _____. They might respond to aggression or repay the kindness they receive.

Unit 5 J.K. Rowling's Impact

Vocabulary

A **Match the words with their correct meanings.**

poverty	generation	found	pop culture	generosity

1 to start an organization   _____

2 the state of being very poor   _____

3 a group of people born around the same time _____

4 the state of being kind and giving   _____

5 art and beliefs that are popular at a given time _____

B **Choose the words from the box to complete the sentences.**

fanfiction	generation	merchandise	charity

1 The bookstore clerk put the _____ on display.

2 The author held a _____ writing contest online.

3 The younger _____ loves fantasy and adventure stories.

4 The _____ raises money and donates books to schools.

Translation

C **Read the sentences and translate them into your language.**

1 Whether they watch the films, read the books, visit *Harry Potter* theme parks, or purchase Hogwarts merchandise, people of all ages can enjoy the world and characters.

→ _____

2 Joanne Rowling, known as J.K. Rowling, didn't always have a glamorous life.

→ _____

3 *Harry Potter* turned into a pop culture phenomenon.

→ _____

Paraphrasing

D **Paraphrase the sentences from the passage with the words in the box.**

passed away	well liked	deter
positively	foundations	giving

1 While she wrote the first *Harry Potter* novel, her mother died suddenly.

→ When writing the first *Harry Potter* book, her mother _____ unexpectedly.

2 She used her success for good by donating to many charities.

→ She used her success _____ by giving to many _____.

3 Rowling's generosity caused her to lose her billionaire status, but that didn't stop her.

→ Rowling's _____ nature made her lose her status as a billionaire, but that didn't _____ her.

4 Decades later, *Harry Potter* remains popular.

→ Many years later, *Harry Potter* continues to be _____.

Listening

E **Listen to the summary and fill in the blanks.**

People of all ages enjoy *Harry Potter*, but who is J.K. Rowling, the author behind this famous brand? J.K. Rowling was living in ❶ _____ when she wrote *Harry Potter*. However, she never gave up, and the books brought her huge success. Rowling used her ❷ _____ for good and donated a lot of ❸ _____. She even founded her own ❹ _____. *Harry Potter* turned into a pop culture phenomenon. Fans dreamed of ❺ _____ Hogwarts. Decades later, the books remain ❻ _____ among readers of all ages.

Unit 6 From Science Fiction to Science Fact

Vocabulary

A **Match the words with their correct meanings.**

novel	imagine	predict	wireless	purchase

1 to make a guess about the future _____

2 to think of _____

3 a long work of fiction _____

4 without wires or cords _____

5 to buy _____

B **Choose the words from the box to complete the sentences.**

purchase	gadgets	reality	design

1 The author included a _____ for a new type of airplane.

2 Her dream of publishing a book became a _____.

3 Science fiction stories often include many unique _____.

4 Do you know where to _____ copies of his new series?

Translation

C **Read the sentences and translate them into your language.**

1 Sometimes, these ideas inspire inventors who turn them into a reality.

→ _____

2 Verne's work inspired Simon Lake, who worked for the US navy.

→ _____

3 Today, people use earbuds to listen to music or even make phone calls.

→ _____

Paraphrasing

D **Paraphrase the sentences from the passage with the words in the box.**

paper	concepts	guessed
device	right	engaging

1 These gadgets make stories more exciting.

→ These inventions make stories more _____ .

2 Sometimes, these ideas inspire inventors who turn them into a reality.

→ Sometimes, these _____ inspire inventors who make them real.

3 In an essay, he predicted that cars would have robot brains.

→ In a _____ , he _____ that cars would possess robot brains.

4 This gadget sent sound directly into the ear.

→ This _____ sent sound waves _____ into an ear.

Listening

E **Listen to the summary and fill in the blanks.**

Science fiction authors imagine new gadgets. Sometimes, these ideas inspire
❶ _____ . Jules Verne wrote about a ❷ _____ that was
powered by electricity. His work inspired Simon Lake to ❸ _____ a
submarine in 1894. Over 50 years ago, Isaac Asimov wrote about cars with robot
❹ _____ . Many companies are testing self-driving cars now. These cars may
be on the ❺ _____ soon. Ray Bradbury wrote about a ❻ _____
that sent sound into the ear. This idea is similar to earbuds.

Unit 7 **Floating Trash Islands**

Vocabulary

A Match the words with their correct meanings.

remove	accumulate	reduce	piece	drift

1 to gather in one place _____

2 to float _____

3 a small part of something _____

4 to take out _____

5 to lower an amount _____

B Choose the words from the box to complete the sentences.

island	solve	devastating	reduce

1 Cutting down forests can be _____ for animal species.

2 The storm caused a lot of damage to the _____ .

3 It is important to _____ the amount of trash we make.

4 Scientists hope to _____ the problem of air pollution.

Translation

C Read the sentences and translate them into your language.

1 Approximately 2.4 million tonnes of plastic makes its way into the oceans every year.

→ _____

2 Another patch of ocean garbage can be found in the Atlantic Ocean.

→ _____

3 Wildlife organizations are working on ways to safely remove the plastic.

→ _____

Paraphrasing

D   **Paraphrase the sentences from the passage with the words in the box.**

transport	increasingly	collected
the size of	numerous	consuming

1 More and more, this trash ends up in rivers, which carry the plastic directly to Earth's oceans.

→ _____, this trash gets into rivers, which _____ the plastic straight into Earth's oceans.

2 This trash has accumulated and formed floating islands of garbage.

→ This garbage has _____ and grew into floating islands of junk.

3 Currently, the island is three times bigger than France.

→ Right now, the island is three times _____ France.

4 Many marine animals die after eating plastic.

→ _____ ocean creatures die after _____ plastic.

Listening

E   **Listen to the summary and fill in the blanks.**

Plastic trash has ❶ _____ in oceans and formed islands of garbage. The Great Pacific Garbage Patch is the largest of these ❷ _____ . It can be found ❸ _____ between California and Hawaii. It's three times bigger than France and grows ❹ _____ each year. Plastic is devastating to ❺ _____ life, but there may be a way to solve the problem. We can reduce the amount of ❻ _____ we use as well as clean up the oceans.

Unit 8 **Desertification**

Vocabulary

A **Match the words with their correct meanings.**

sustainable	hunger	flood	graze	major

1 to eat grass and plants _____

2 important or significant _____

3 a feeling caused by a lack of food _____

4 when land becomes covered in water _____

5 not using up resources _____

B **Choose the words from the box to complete the sentences.**

man-made	sustainable	natural disasters	drought

1 Hurricanes and tornadoes are examples of _____ .

2 Solar and wind power are _____ forms of energy.

3 The _____ killed many animals when they could not find water.

4 Some lakes are not formed naturally but are _____ .

Translation

C **Read the sentences and translate them into your language.**

1 Deserts form when land loses its water, plants, and wildlife.

→ _____

2 Food prices will increase along with poverty and hunger.

→ _____

3 New technology may bring life and water back to deserts.

→ _____

16

Paraphrasing

D **Paraphrase the sentences from the passage with the words in the box.**

location	absence	occur
turn into	allow	frequently

1 Much of the world's land may become deserts in the near future.

→ A lot of the world's land might _____ deserts in the coming years.

2 Sometimes, farmers let too many animals graze in one area.

→ At times, farmers _____ too many animals to graze in one _____.

3 As Earth warms, droughts occur more often.

→ As Earth gets hotter, droughts happen more _____.

4 Without plants, floods and dust storms will happen more often.

→ In the _____ of plants, floods and dust storms will _____ more regularly.

Listening

E **Listen to the summary and fill in the blanks.**

Deserts form when land loses its water, plants, and ❶ _____. Man-made activities and climate change cause areas to become ❷ _____. When this happens, farming becomes more difficult and ❸ _____ will increase. Additionally, drinking water will no longer be as safe. ❹ _____, like floods, might also happen more frequently. Laws, ❺ _____, and technology can help prevent desertification. In some cases, desertification can be ❻ _____. New technology could help bring water back to dry areas.

Unit 9 Plants that Stink

Vocabulary

A **Match the words with their correct meanings.**

rot	lure	pollen	trap	survive

1 to attract   _____

2 to break down   _____

3 to capture   _____

4 a powdery substance that comes from a plant   _____

5 to not die   _____

B **Choose the words from the box to complete the sentences.**

normally	disgusting	survive	seeds

1 In his opinion, leafy vegetables taste _____.

2 The gardener planted the _____ several centimeters apart.

3 _____, plants do not grow much during winter.

4 How do cacti _____ in the hot desert sun?

Translation

C **Read the sentences and translate them into your language.**

1 When we think of flowers, we often imagine sweet scents that lure insects.

   ➔ _____

2 Native to the rainforests of Sumatra in Indonesia, it can grow up to 3 meters tall.

   ➔ _____

3 As its name suggests, the Dead Horse Arum Lily smells like a dead horse.

   ➔ _____

Paraphrasing

D **Paraphrase the sentences from the passage with the words in the box.**

decaying	stenches	usually
generates	drawn	coats

1 But some flowering plants produce terrible smells.

→ However, some flower-bearing plants make awful _____.

2 It got this name because it produces a smell that's similar to rotting meat.

→ It was given this name because it _____ a stink that's similar to _____ meat.

3 Beetles and flies, which normally feed on decaying flesh, are attracted to this smell.

→ Beetles and flies, which _____ eat rotting flesh, are _____ to this smell.

4 Over the course of a day, it covers the flies in pollen.

→ As the day goes by, it _____ the flies in pollen.

Listening

E **Listen to the summary and fill in the blanks.**

Some plants produce ❶ _____ smells that attract insects. The Titan Arum is native to Indonesia. It smells similar to ❷ _____ meat. Beetles and ❸ _____ are attracted to this smell. The Stinking Corpse Lily also grows in Indonesia. Forest animals are ❹ _____ to its rotting meat smell. Similarly, the Dead Horse Arum Lily smells like a dead horse. This flower traps flies and ❺ _____ them in pollen. The flies carry the pollen to other flowers, which ensures the plant ❻ _____.

Unit 10 **Plant Growing Seasons**

Vocabulary

A   **Match the words with their correct meanings.**

stem	portion	single	period	life cycle

1 an amount of time   _____

2 one   _____

3 the time from birth to death   _____

4 the main body of a plant   _____

5 a piece of a larger whole   _____

B   **Choose the words from the box to complete the sentences.**

roots	rare	portion	shrub

1 The garden includes ten different species of _____.

2 The tree's _____ have spread beneath the street and building.

3 A _____ of the plant will die and fall off in cold weather.

4 Only found on one continent, this plant is very _____.

Translation

C   **Read the sentences and translate them into your language.**

1 Many common garden flowers are classified as annuals.

➡ _____

2 By the end of the second growing season, they begin to die.

➡ _____

3 Plants that live for many years are called perennials.

➡ _____

Paraphrasing

D **Paraphrase the sentences from the passage with the words in the box.**

instance	survive	each
period	need	usually

1 But some rare species can live for several thousand years.

→ However, some unique species can _____ for several thousand years.

2 Marigolds, for example, complete their life cycle in a single growing season.

→ Marigolds, for _____, finish their life cycle in one growing _____.

3 They require up to two years to complete their entire life cycle.

→ They _____ up to two years to finish their whole life cycle.

4 Typically, they produce seeds every year, but they do not die after.

→ _____, they make seeds _____ year, but they do not die afterwards.

Listening

E **Listen to the summary and fill in the blanks.**

There are three classifications for plants: ❶ _____, biennial, and perennial. First, annuals live for a single growing ❷ _____ before they die. Many common garden flowers are annuals. Biennials, on the other hand, grow for two seasons before they begin to ❸ _____. Onions and carrots are ❹ _____. Finally, plants that live for many years are ❺ _____ as perennials. These plants produce seeds every year but don't die after. Only part of a perennial dies in winter and then grows back in ❻ _____.

Unit 11 **The First Currencies**

Vocabulary

A **Match the words with their correct meanings.**

barter	emerge	debt	service	valuable

1 to trade goods or services without money　　_____

2 money owed　　_____

3 to appear　　_____

4 having a lot of worth　　_____

5 work done for someone　　_____

B **Choose the words from the box to complete the sentences.**

debts	weapons	manufacture	bartered

1 The company decided to _____ electric cars.

2 Early humans traded food, fur, and _____.

3 She had many _____ after receiving loans from the bank.

4 The woman _____ food for cleaning services.

Translation

C **Read the sentences and translate them into your language.**

1 Before we had money, people got what they needed by trading.

➡ _____

2 Sometimes a person could trade one cow for two or more goats.

➡ _____

3 They were nearly impossible to forge, which made them an attractive option.

➡ _____

Paraphrasing

D **Paraphrase the sentences from the passage with the words in the box.**

worth	grew to be	exchanged
as a result	approximately	form of money

1 Thus, trading cattle became an important part of human life.

→ _____ , trading cattle _____ a valuable part of human life.

2 Cows were considered more valuable than goats.

→ Cows were thought to be _____ more than goats.

3 Around three thousand years ago, cowrie shells emerged as a currency.

→ _____ three thousand years ago, cowrie shells appeared as a _____ .

4 Cowrie shells were traded for items and services.

→ Cowrie shells were _____ for goods and services.

Listening

E **Listen to the summary and fill in the blanks.**

Before we had money, people got what they needed by ❶ _____ . This system had many flaws, so currency began to ❷ _____ trade. As cattle was important to early humans, it became the first ❸ _____ . Around 3,000 years ago, cowrie shells emerged as an attractive currency ❹ _____ . These shells were traded for items and services. In 1000 BC, China began to make ❺ _____ shells and later made a flat version. Soon, other societies also began using metals to make ❻ _____ .

Unit 12 Paradox of Value

Vocabulary

A Match the words with their correct meanings.

strand	abundant	quality	gem	urgency

1 a stone with a high value   _____

2 large in quantity   _____

3 the need for fast action   _____

4 of a high standard   _____

5 to cause someone to get stuck somewhere   _____

B Choose the words from the box to complete the sentences.

essential	logically	market price	quality

1 Resources, such as food and water, are _____ for survival.

2 The _____ of tomatoes rose after the terrible storm.

3 _____, people should value food over gems.

4 The company is known for making _____ products.

Translation

C Read the sentences and translate them into your language.

1 Since water is more useful, it should naturally have a higher market price.

➡ _____

2 Most people have steady access to clean water.

➡ _____

3 Once survival is no longer an issue, the man will again pay more for diamonds.

➡ _____

Paraphrasing

D **Paraphrase the sentences from the passage with the words in the box.**

a lack of	instead	overturns
tougher	are willing to	deemed

1 Rather, many non-essential resources are considered valuable.

➡ _____, many unnecessary resources are _____ valuable.

2 People will pay thousands of dollars for a single stone.

➡ People _____ pay thousands of dollars for one stone.

3 It is much more difficult to find quality diamonds.

➡ It is much _____ to locate diamonds of a good quality.

4 When water is in short supply, the diamond-water paradox often reverses.

➡ When there is _____ water, the diamond-water paradox frequently

_____.

Listening

E **Listen to the summary and fill in the blanks.**

Many non-essential resources are considered ❶ _____. This is called the
Paradox of Value. Humans need water to ❷ _____. Naturally, it should have a
higher price. However, gems like diamonds ❸ _____ much more. This occurs
because people have ❹ _____ access to clean water, which lowers the
sense of urgency to find it. ❺ _____, however, are rare. This drives up the
market price of diamonds. The diamond-water paradox can reverse. A man dying of
❻ _____ will value water much more than diamonds.

Unit 13 John William Waterhouse

Vocabulary

A **Match the words with their correct meanings.**

showcase	character	myth	artistic	dreamy

1 having skill in the arts _____

2 to display _____

3 having dream-like qualities _____

4 a person in a story _____

5 a story explaining something about the ancient world _____

B **Choose the words from the box to complete the sentences.**

inspired	nature	showcase	style

1 The artist's _____ stayed the same for many years.

2 The beautiful sunset _____ the painter.

3 The art gallery will _____ the *Mona Lisa*.

4 Monet commonly painted scenes from _____.

Translation

C **Read the sentences and translate them into your language.**

1 Born in 1849, Waterhouse grew up in an artistic family.

→ _____

2 His work started to feature fields, forests, and lakes.

→ _____

3 Waterhouse's Ophelia paintings are his most famous.

→ _____

Paraphrasing

D **Paraphrase the sentences from the passage with the words in the box.**

the natural world	depicted	lovely
prior to	vibrant	was raised

1 Waterhouse grew up in an artistic family.

→ Waterhouse _____ in a creative family.

2 Before Raphael, artists mostly painted nature.

→ _____ Raphael, artists usually painted _____ .

3 He used bright colors and often included beautiful women.

→ He employed _____ hues and frequently included _____ women.

4 Usually, she is shown sitting by the water just before her death.

→ Typically, she is _____ sitting by the water right before she dies.

Listening

E **Listen to the summary and fill in the blanks.**

> John William Waterhouse was a popular English painter. He studied ❶ _____
> art. However, his style changed over time. Waterhouse began to paint ❷ _____
> scenes of nature. He may have been ❸ _____ by the pre-Raphaelite
> Brotherhood. The Brotherhood disliked classical art. They wanted to return to an older
> ❹ _____ . Waterhouse also painted ❺ _____ from myths and
> literature. He especially ❻ _____ painting Ophelia.

Unit 14 Japan's Digital Art Gallery

Vocabulary

A **Match the words with their correct meanings.**

bind	projector	lantern	permanent	feature

1 to restrict _____

2 long-term _____

3 a machine that shines light and images _____

4 to show something as an important part _____

5 a type of lamp _____

B **Choose the words from the box to complete the sentences.**

permanent	social media	wander	digital

1 The artists formed a group on _____.

2 His _____ art is sold in many online shops.

3 The students were allowed to _____ in the gallery.

4 The statue will have a _____ home in the park.

Translation

C **Read the sentences and translate them into your language.**

1 As technology changes, so does art.

→ _____

2 One gallery has taken digital art to the next level.

→ _____

3 There are no tour guides or paths to follow. Visitors are free to wander.

→ _____

Paraphrasing

D **Paraphrase the sentences from the passage with the words in the box.**

identical	devote	alters
exhibited	wish	different from

1 Technology also affects how art is displayed.

→ Technology _____ the way art is _____, too.

2 TeamLab Borderless is unlike any gallery in the world.

→ TeamLab Borderless is _____ other galleries around the world.

3 They can spend as much time as they like in their favorite scenes.

→ They can _____ as much time as they _____ to their favorite scenes.

4 The art is always moving, so no two photographs are ever the same.

→ The artwork is always shifting, so no two pictures are ever _____.

Listening

E **Listen to the summary and fill in the blanks.**

Art galleries are becoming more exciting with ❶ _____. A group called teamLab founded a digital art ❷ _____ in Tokyo. The building is large and has many rooms. There are hundreds of computers and ❸ _____ inside. They shine images on the floors, walls, and ceilings. Many of the rooms feature images of ❹ _____. The scenes are always changing, so each visitor has a ❺ _____ experience. Visitors are encouraged to take ❻ _____ and share them on social media.

Unit 15 Emotional Support Animals

Vocabulary

A **Match the words with their correct meanings.**

cope with	trauma	bond	react	reliable

1 to deal with _____

2 mental harm caused by a bad situation _____

3 able to be trusted _____

4 to form a relationship _____

5 to respond _____

B **Choose the words from the box to complete the sentences.**

disorder	bonded	affectionate	behave

1 The girl developed a dangerous bone _____.

2 Some rabbits can be very gentle and _____.

3 It is important to _____ well during social events.

4 The students _____ with their second-grade teacher.

Translation

C **Read the sentences and translate them into your language.**

1 These days, some people are turning to animals in their time of need.

→ _____

2 Dogs are reliable and bond well with humans.

→ _____

3 Unlike most working animals, support animals don't need special training.

→ _____

Paraphrasing

D Paraphrase the sentences from the passage with the words in the box.

well-being		suitable	likewise
damage	coping		form friendships

1 These events can harm a person's mental health.

→ Events like these can _____ someone's mental _____.

2 People living with trauma may have a hard time making friends.

→ People who have trauma might struggle to _____.

3 Similarly, a person with a mental disorder may have trouble dealing with stress.

→ _____, a person who has a mental disorder could have difficulty _____ with stress.

4 Not all pets make good support animals.

→ Not all pets make _____ therapy animals.

Listening

E Listen to the summary and fill in the blanks.

Certain events can harm a person's mental health. These days, people are turning to ❶ _____ to cope with their feelings. Emotional support animals can offer friendship and ❷ _____. Dogs tend to make the best support animals. However, many cats have also become support animals in ❸ _____ years. Sometimes, horses, ❹ _____, and birds are also chosen. Support animals don't need any special training. But the animal must be very ❺ _____ and sensitive to an owner's ❻ _____.

Unit 16 **Phobias**

Vocabulary

A **Match the words with their correct meanings.**

report	needle	open space	rapid	symptom

1 a large area without walls _____

2 a physical reaction _____

3 very fast _____

4 to tell _____

5 a tool used to give an injection _____

B **Choose the words from the box to complete the sentences.**

fear	excessive	intensify	symptom

1 The disease's symptoms will _____ over time.

2 Some people have a _____ of lakes and oceans.

3 He spent an _____ amount of money.

4 One _____ of the flu is a high fever.

Translation

C **Read the sentences and translate them into your language.**

1 Having fears is a normal part of life.

→ _____

2 There are many symptoms associated with phobias.

→ _____

3 For example, fear of flying can make traveling very hard.

→ _____

Paraphrasing

D Paraphrase the sentences from the passage with the words in the box.

are afraid of	vomit	going to
prevent	confronted by	tremble

1 As children, many people fear spiders or ghosts.

→ When they are children, a lot of people _____ spiders or ghosts.

2 When faced with a fear, some people have an extreme reaction.

→ When _____ a fear, some people experience an overreaction.

3 Some people may shake or feel sick to their stomach.

→ Some people might _____ or feel as though they will _____.

4 A fear of needles or blood can stop someone from visiting a hospital.

→ A fear of needles or blood could _____ a person from _____ a hospital.

Listening

E Listen to the summary and fill in the blanks.

Fears are normal, but some people may be ❶ _____ from a phobia.
Phobias cause an excessive amount of fear about a situation or ❷ _____.
When faced with the object or situation, people have an extreme ❸ _____.
These symptoms are unpleasant and may cause the phobia to get ❹ _____.
Common phobias often involve ❺ _____ or health care. Some people might
also fear storms or everyday ❻ _____, such as flying. These phobias make
life very difficult.

Further
Writing Practice

Unit 1　The Fiery Crater

Q **Which famous geological formation do you want to visit? What would you like to do there?**

A　The following table shows some ideas for answering the question above. Check the one that you like the most. If you have your own idea, write it in the last row.

Places	Description and Things to Do
☐ Khao Ta Pu in Thailand	• a 20-meter high limestone rock that grows wider at the top • take a boat ride around the rock
☐ Giant's Causeway in Ireland	• 40,000 basalt columns created by cooling lava • walk along the trails and enjoy the scenery
☐ Horseshoe Bend in Arizona, USA	• a horseshoe-shaped gorge made by the Colorado River • see the amazing colors at sunrise or take a raft ride

B　Read the question again and complete the following paragraph.

If I could visit a famous geological formation, I would like to go to _____

_____. It is _____

_____. I would like to _____

_____.

Unit 2 **Geothermal Energy**

Q **Choose a type of clean and sustainable energy. What are the features and benefits?**

A The following table shows some ideas for answering the question above. Check the one that you like the most. If you have your own idea, write it in the last row.

Type of Energy	Features and Benefits
☐ Solar Energy	• energy gathered by solar panels and stored in cells • can be installed cheaply on buildings
☐ Wind Energy	• energy gathered when wind spins a turbine • can be installed on farms and doesn't pollute the air
☐ Biomass Energy	• energy that comes from plants • can be used to make fuel for cars and power plants

B Read the question again and complete the following paragraph.

_____ is a form of clean, sustainable energy.

It is _____.

This energy system _____

_____.

Unit 3 The Red Panda

Q **Choose an endangered species. Research some facts and write about the animal.**

A   The following table shows some ideas for answering the question above. Check the one that you like the most. If you have your own idea, write it in the last row.

Animal	Habitat and Population
☐ Siberian Tiger	• native to Northeast China and Eastern Russia • around 500 Siberian tigers living in the wild
☐ Blue Whale	• a marine animal that lives in Earth's oceans • between 10,000 and 25,000 blue whales living in the oceans
☐ Steller Sea Lion	• found in the North Pacific Ocean near coastal areas • fewer than 50,000 Steller sea lions left in the world

B   Read the question again and complete the following paragraph.

The _____ is an endangered animal.

It is _____.

There are _____

_____.

Unit 4 Crow Intelligence

Q   **Think of an especially intelligent animal and write about it.**

A   The following table shows some ideas for answering the question above. Check the one that you like the most. If you have your own idea, write it in the last row.

Animal	Features and Abilities
☐ Dolphin	• has a large brain that is designed for underwater communication • can solve problems and show signs of emotions
☐ Elephant	• has a brain similar to humans and an excellent memory • show signs of self-awareness and many emotions
☐ Chimpanzee	• shares almost 99% of its DNA with humans • can use tools and remember numbers

B   Read the question again and complete the following paragraph.

The _____ is an especially intelligent animal.

It _____.

These animals _____

_____.

Unit 5 J.K. Rowling's Impact

What is your favorite fairy tale? What is it about?

A The following table shows some ideas for answering the question above. Check the one that you like the most. If you have your own idea, write it in the last row.

Fairy Tale	Characters and Story
☐ *Snow White and the Seven Dwarves*	• a young princess and seven dwarves • Snow White escapes an evil queen and hides in a cottage
☐ *Cinderella*	• a girl, her evil stepmother, and two stepsisters • Cinderella goes to the ball with the help of her fairy godmother
☐ *Jack and the Beanstalk*	• a boy, a giant, and a magic hen • Jack climbs a magic beanstalk to the clouds and defeats the giant

B Read the question again and complete the following paragraph.

My favorite fairy tale is _____.

It is about _____.

In this story, _____

_____.

Unit 6 From Science Fiction to Science Fact

Q **What is your favorite science fiction film? Write about the setting and plot.**

A The following table shows some ideas for answering the question above. Check the one that you like the most. If you have your own idea, write it in the last row.

Film	Setting and Plot
☐ *E.T.* (Universal Pictures)	• in a small town in America • a young boy helps a lost alien call home
☐ *Wall-E* (Disney)	• on a futuristic Earth that's polluted with trash • a robot helps humans return to Earth from space
☐ *Big Hero 6* (Disney)	• in a fictional city called San Fransokyo • a grieving boy forms a team of superheroes

B Read the question again and complete the following paragraph.

My favorite science fiction film is _____.

It takes place _____.

In this movie, _____

_____.

Unit 7 **Floating Trash Islands**

Q   **Write about one way you can reduce the amount of pollution you make.**

A   The following table shows some ideas for answering the question above. Check the one that you like the most. If you have your own idea, write it in the last row.

Method	Benefits
☐ Use Reusable Shopping Bags	• reduces the number of plastic bags I use • helps reduce the amount of plastic that gets into oceans
☐ Turn off Lights and Electronics	• lowers the amount of energy I consume • helps prevent dangerous air pollution
☐ Take the Bus with My Family	• reduces the number of cars on the road • helps reduce gases that cause global warming

B   Read the question again and complete the following paragraph.

To reduce pollution, I can _____.

This method _____.

It also _____.

_____.

Unit 8 Desertification

Q **Write about a serious threat to the environment. What are the effects and solutions?**

A   The following table shows some ideas for answering the question above. Check the one that you like the most. If you have your own idea, write it in the last row.

Problem	Effects and Solutions
☐ Global Warming	• causes polar ice to melt and natural disasters to increase • reducing greenhouse gases and using clean energy
☐ An Oil Spill	• poisons water supplies and kills marine life • lowering the number of water-related accidents
☐ Deforestation	• destroys animal habitats and lowers oxygen production • preventing logging and planting more trees

B   Read the question again and complete the following paragraph.

One serious environmental threat is _____.

It _____.

To solve this problem, we can start by _____

_____.

Unit 9 **Plants that Stink**

Q   **Think of a unique plant. Write about its special features.**

A   The following table shows some ideas for answering the question above. Check the one that you like the most. If you have your own idea, write it in the last row.

Plant	Features
☐ Venus Flytrap	• a carnivorous plant that eats insects • snaps closed when bugs land on its leaves
☐ Baobab Tree	• a tree that grows in dry areas of Africa • contains a lot of water, so people call it the "Tree of Life"
☐ Pitcher Plant	• a carnivorous plant that's shaped like a pitcher • eats insects, spiders, worms, and even lizards

B   Read the question again and complete the following paragraph.

The _____ is a very unique plant.

It is _____.

This plant _____

_____.

Unit 10 **Plant Growing Seasons**

Q **What is your favorite flowering plant? Describe its life cycle and appearance.**

A The following table shows some ideas for answering the question above. Check the one that you like the most. If you have your own idea, write it in the last row.

Flowering Plant	Life Cycle and Appearance
☐ Peonies	• perennials native to Asia, Europe, and North America • large colorful blooms ranging from pale pink to dark red
☐ Tulips	• spring-blooming perennials found in many countries • brightly colored flowers, usually red, pink, yellow, or white
☐ Marigolds	• annuals that bloom all summer before dying • yellow or golden flowers that grow to be 4–6 cm wide

B Read the question again and complete the following paragraph.

_____ are my favorite flowering plants.

They are _____.

They have _____

_____.

Unit 11 The First Currencies

Write about a method of payment your parents often use. What are some benefits and problems?

A   The following table shows some ideas for answering the question above. Check the one that you like the most. If you have your own idea, write it in the last row.

Method	Benefits and Problems
☐ Credit Cards	• convenient and easy to use online and in stores • credit card numbers can be stolen easily
☐ Cash	• easy to spend and give away to others • thefts can happen when people carry too much cash
☐ Online Banking	• convenient for paying bills and sending funds • it cannot be used to buy things in some stores

B   Read the question again and complete the following paragraph.

My parents mostly use _____ as a payment method.

This method is good because it's _____

_____. However, _____

_____ .

46

Unit 12 **Paradox of Value**

Q **If you had a lot of money, what would you buy?**

A The following table shows some ideas for answering the question above. Check the one that you like the most. If you have your own idea, write it in the last row.

Item	Reasons
☐ A House	• a big home with many rooms and a swimming pool • my whole family could live there with me
☐ A Sports Car	• a luxury car that can drive very fast • I would learn to drive and take trips with my friends
☐ A Diamond Necklace	• a beautiful piece of jewelry with many diamonds • I could wear it to special events and impress others

B Read the question again and complete the following paragraph.

If I had a lot of money, I would buy _____.

I really want _____.

Also, _____
_____.

Unit 13 John William Waterhouse

Q Who is your favorite artist? What is his or her most famous artwork?

A The following table shows some ideas for answering the question above. Check the one that you like the most. If you have your own idea, write it in the last row.

Artist	Life and Most Famous Work
☐ Leonardo da Vinci	• an Italian painter who lived from 1452 to 1519 • the *Mona Lisa*, a painting of a mysterious smiling woman
☐ Vincent van Gogh	• a Dutch painter who created over 2,000 artworks • *The Starry Night*, a dreamy painting of the night sky
☐ Salvador Dali	• a Spanish painter who died in 1989 • *The Persistence of Memory*, a painting of melting clocks

B Read the question again and complete the following paragraph.

My favorite artist is _____.

He/She is/was _____.

His/Her most famous work is _____

_____.

Unit 14 Japan's Digital Art Gallery

Q **Write about an art gallery you want to visit. What would you like to see there?**

A The following table shows some ideas for answering the question above. Check the one that you like the most. If you have your own idea, write it in the last row.

Gallery	Location and Things to See
☐ The Louvre	• the world's largest art museum, located in Paris, France • see famous works of art and enjoy the architecture
☐ The Museum of Modern Art	• a modern art gallery located in New York City • see the modern paintings and sculptures on display
☐ The National Gallery	• a gallery in London that houses many masterpieces • view works by Raphael, Michelangelo, and many more

B Read the question again and complete the following paragraph.

I want to visit _____.

It is _____.

I would like to _____

_____.

Unit 15 **Emotional Support Animals**

What is the best way to deal with stress?

A The following table shows some ideas for answering the question above. Check the one that you like the most. If you have your own idea, write it in the last row.

Method	How to Do It and Benefits
☐ Meditation	• sit in a quiet place and try to empty your mind • reduce your heart rate and lower stress hormones
☐ Doing Art	• try to express yourself through painting, music, or writing • help you understand your feelings and make choices
☐ Exercising	• increase your heart rate by running, jogging, or swimming • lower your anger level and help you feel happier

B Read the question again and complete the following paragraph.

I think the best way to deal with stress is _____.

You should _____.

This can _____

_____.

Unit 16 Phobias

Q **Write about a fear you have. Why are you afraid of this thing?**

A The following table shows some ideas for answering the question above. Check the one that you like the most. If you have your own idea, write it in the last row.

Fear	Reaction and Reason
☐ Public Speaking	• my heart rate increases and I sweat a lot • I worry about making mistakes in front of others
☐ Snakes	• I scream and run away as fast as possible • I think snakes are deadly when they bite someone
☐ Sharks	• I am unable to swim in open water • I have heard sharks will attack humans

B Read the question again and complete the following paragraph.

One of my greatest fears is _____ .

When faced with this fear, _____ .

I have this fear because _____

_____ .

MEMO

Fundamental Reading

BASIC 1